Philippe Beck

Didactic Poetries

Translated by Nicola Marae Allain
Preface by Jean-Luc Nancy

Table of Contents

Acknowledgments

I am deeply indebted to Philippe Beck for granting me the privilege to undertake the delicate work of translating his complex, exquisite poems. Philippe generously responded to my queries, collaborated closely on the first series of poems completed for the book, and consistently championed this translation. Mr. Gérard Tessier graciously reviewed the poetry translations in progress, and assisted with the resolution of some challenging ambiguities. My husband Joseph Bruchac patiently provided a poet's ear to listen to early drafts, and suggested the occasional turn of phrase for the "right choice" of words. My son Mikaël was steadfast in his support and encouragement over the years I devoted to this project. I would like to thank Drew Burk, Jason Wagner, and the editorial team at Univocal Publishing for believing in this project, and bringing this work to life. I take full responsibility for any errors or omissions.

I am grateful to the Office of Academic Affairs, my deans and colleagues at SUNY Empire State College for continuously supporting me in this endeavor, and hosting Philippe Beck readings of the work in progress in 2011 and 2015. The readings were also sponsored by the Cultural Services of the French Embassy in New York, with assistance from the Institut français.

Nicola Marae Allain, Ph. D.
Saratoga Springs, NY

Accelerated Sublime

If I say that Philippe Beck's *Didactic Poetries* is a sublime book, I am not making a judgment of taste, but of philosophical philology, for in this way I remind us that the didactic poem is, according to Kant, one of the three possible artistic modalities for presenting the sublime. The two others are tragedy in verse and oratorio. For Kant, the sublime represents the sentiment of reason that experiences within both the limit of its capacity for representation and, aligned with the affect itself, going beyond this limit: a suspension beyond forms. In truth, here reason touches upon its innermost strength: its demand for the unconditioned, its connection constantly reaching towards depth or towards the summit, which are withheld. The sublime culminates in an *apatheia*, in an imperceptible affect wherein the intensity resonates within the emptiness of principles and ends where, beginning with Kant, the secular space of metaphysics widens.

The arts of the sublime — composed arts, as Kant underlines — therefore have the task of presenting this negative presentation, or this presentation of the negative, or this presenting negative. This is why the three are composed of a form (dramatic scene, music, versification) and of an exercise in language: that is, of an attempt at meaning, or truth. All three are ways of formulating a thought. The form of thought has occupied thinking since it was thought, which means once it went beyond contemplation or participation (which may never have rigorously happened). This establishes a manifest community between the three forms which may reach the point of making them osmotic or symbiotic. Nevertheless, we are no longer in Romanticism (despite what we think), and traces of types must remain even within a combined or composed genre.

The specific feature of the didactic poem is to teach, to transmit (a) knowledge. The transmission of knowledge is the least transmissible thing — we know this well (and this "knowing well" in itself is only transmitted blindly). In fact knowledge is not accessible; it is accessible to itself, within itself or towards itself, depending on what occurs during an exchange.

And so Beck opens with:

> *What must be said*
> *is not already spoken*
> *in the individual's brain,*
> *nor in the Collective,*
> *but it is said because*
> *of the conversation*
> *which creates necessity*
> *all around brains* (23)

He reveals his intentions: the didactic will be the discussion opening between him and the reader, being open from him to himself, being that distance across which "the ear sends itself letters" (126). One needs separation, sending, address, and this in itself defines both poetry and teaching: the poem teaches. What does it teach? That which you will know how to learn if you allow yourself to be taught, which is to fold, unfold, open according to this space for exchange: between yours and mine, where "the big I is absent" (23) (this book teaches a theory on the subject of enunciation, of the subject who begins to speak, and who is "space" or "X" (212) or "The radical idiot" (214) and of the subject who carries himself this way, one step ahead of him, he the same and he the other, the other that doesn't understand himself yet and who must learn about himself).

> *and space is the beginning poem*

he says (130) in an alexandrine rare enough that it needs to be highlighted (part of the instruction, no doubt). That means that the concern is the form of thinking as versification, or as "reversal" (118).

But on the other hand, the thinking in question, as thinking about knowledge that isn't packaged, isn't something other than philosophy. We learn this through the text (I'll come back to that), but we learn it first through Kant, and by this, that Kant doesn't say, but is thinking nonetheless, that the only didactic poem worthy of the name in our entire history is the one written by Lucretius: thus philosophical and *of the nature of things*, thus physical, physically metaphysical.

Democritus shows through here, he is shown laughing because he sees our theatre:

> *When all is dust, and adds to the dust,*
> *but atom theory,*
> *empty and infinite.* (189)

Where "theory" refers in one work to Democritus's thinking as taken up by Lucretius and the free falling succession of atoms in the void: theory1 of atomic theory2. Yet this in a poem, what does this mean, and why this *hapax* of poetry and of philosophy (for there is nothing to say about other attempts at didactic poetry), for which Kant discreetly activates the memory (Kant to whom Democritus, Epicurus and Lucretius constantly refer the subject of pleasure, which is always sensory: thus the sublime is sentiment, and reason cannot help but physically be felt in passing, even in an irreversible coma, from where perhaps it always originates and returns).

(Here, you may notice, the atomic dust mixes with biblical pulverulence, flesh returning to the earth. But this is neither Greek, nor Jewish; here it is another philosophy which constantly didactates: the "last man" who "blinks," "temporary blindness" for a "community of blind knowledge"(143). Here the teacher and the taught is not a humanist man, not a superman, not a divine man, but a last man who laughs. Democritus laughs, and also laughs the title of "didactic poetries" (with its plural, one must also note the plural…).

But why, yes, why? If not because precisely this thinking, this theory, is linked of its own accord to a cadenced succession of words: linked to meaning taken within a continuous falling of words across the void and the infinite. This theory attaches itself because it is a thought falling into the void, but in a fall and a void where there is a necessity to grant a form and also attempt skill: Beck takes on what we call nihilism as a renewed possibility for ethics in that which *ethos* would be above all the conduct of language (tight conduct, yet laughing, dry and jerky but restrained).

> *understand that the choice*
> *of specific turns of phrases,*
> *of an inflection*
> *is a matter of mores,*
> *of morality.*
> *A man speaks*
> *to others* (45-46)

And so,

> *Poetry the right choice*
> *of every word attached*
> *rather than attaching* (126)

To the supposed poetic seduction that gets stuck in evocation, he opposes attaching one word against the other according to rules of a "riddlery" (58) which recognizes silence alongside language; in other words that by which knowledge (meaning, truth, if you will) takes effect in language, which means in the physical fabric of thought. This is exactly what Kant wanted while feeling incapable of getting there materially and through speech: to penetrate reason with a precise feeling, clear and poignant with its own impossible infinity (atomizing reason). (One must know it to believe it: Kant regretted not being a poet.)

Consequently, philosophy is defined here as

> *[…] the undefined*
> *endeavor of thinking*
> *of reasons for its destruction*
> *by literature.* (126)

Philosophy is permanently being destroyed by literature, and this destruction has reasons that therefore give reason to philosophy in its essentially destructible constitution. If that which destroys it is "the right choice of words," it is because philosophy is incapable of making the right choice. In fact, it doesn't choose, it takes words for their meaning (so "idea" means "visible form" and puts visibility in the invisible, ideality, which subsequently abandons all forms). In doing so philosophy is not blind: it knows that meaning self-destructs just like an automatic teller machine that one tries to breach. It knows that this self-destruction is the logical foundation of its *logos* (its archilogy, its mythology), and also gives the rule of philosophy itself as essentially destructible: by poetry, by the atomic attaching of words against the immanent continuity of meaning.

Thus, Beck's idiosyncratic versification, his taut reversal, breathless, "antirhythmic," (147) agrees and engages for the reason that:

> *enjoyment or enthusiasm*
> *need a Stop*
> *that doesn't destroy them.* (147)

Actually, he gets carried away endlessly and doesn't stop. He rhythms dryly, tightly, he hammers or briefly reels off, tendentially atomic, marking this tense beat with utmost clarity when the issue is the utmost didactic, the lesson of the constitution of the subject itself.

> *He forces to write anew*
> *so that the progression*
> *in question*
> *(which is the construction*

of the self,
self,
place of general
meeting)
may be vast and smooth (169)

A little further down (or, later) it will be said that "Etna is also a meeting place," concerning Empedocles. Meeting self with self = thinking = being thrust into the lava = falling atoms = exact knowledge of the impossible and necessary contingency, in other words the con-tingency where self touches self doing nothing more than touching itself, precisely = spread, and open this space across which a word notwithstanding with difficulty and decidedly, ironically but seriously, navigates its rough sequences.

There is a speed specific to this touch and this fall, a speed indefinitely accelerated but jerky, as if motionless and hopping (for the Greek hopping, see 132), which speeds from stop to stop as if he were hammering nails one after the other rather than putting one foot in front of the other. It's a *real time* mimetic, of instantaneous communication, a histrionic (see "Amusement," 178) of *feet* contortions (see above, the octosyllable followed by another cut, triggering the jerky tribrach-iamb/lone/ditrochee/ anapest). These feet — beating in place a space (just) slightly open, given over to trampling, like a kind of clay court where one sees a ball bounce and specks of dirt rise and fall — learn with impatience about these forms of thought, of the reason for their senseless effect, of their scanned scansions *et generaliter de natura rerum musicarum.*

Jean-Luc Nancy

In memoriam Georges François Beck

Didactic Poetries

0. Liminal poem

If an I does not begin,
it is because of the sum
of strong concerns
that make and unmake
someone's history
in the history of some ones
in the history of many
and not in everyone's.
For a someone differs
in the sum of possible exchanges
with everyone
(the big I is also
theoretically absent, and
the ordinary you and I
strive to become a You
before the imagined arrival
of the big I
that does not exist);
discussions begin
because of discussions.
What must be said
is not already spoken
in the individual's brain,
nor in the Collective,
but it is said
because of the conversation
which creates necessity
all around brains
and hearts.
And the world is not everyone's
negative rough draft.

1. Rilke

R.,
mirror
of the complex goodness
of the reader
who does not write;
mirror
of the beautiful inadequacy
of he who
puts into words what we do not voice,
what we haven't
said,
and who confirms
the comfort
of a desire for perfection.

A R. plan is not
a threshold stone
that stops the swing
of the door
in the event of an attack
or kidnapping.
Sweat of a spent angel.

A world of complaints
on paper, verbalized,
circused,
suits complainants.
Complainants, these are those
who have something to complain about.
And forgotten lyres in the hands of
contemporaries
have never been
rooted there.
No man is born
with a lyre in hand
and as soon as he acquainted himself
with music

with the general Great Technique,
the lyre nonetheless
did not root in his palm.
But he's a singer
as soon as things go wrong —
the bad beginning in the details.
To sonorous eyes, if need be.

If hell is the place of dispersion,
forever,
then the orphicizers, the neo-,
are lovers of hell
most often without knowing,
for they exalt an exploded world
in exalting Wealth
at all cost.
Even if it is, often, onerous.
Orpheus, the first
wants to experience hell.
But now
do we need *to go* towards hell?
We are there or we have been.
No need to go there to please him.
Nothing pleases him.
He is from the surface.
The non-remark makes do.
Despite the apocalyptists,
or also because of them.
Those who leave beauties behind.
A remark rots too easily.

Ovid asked about Orpheus:
what is the point of fascinating
wild beasts, conquered
with songs?
Would he have entranced
the Roman rope maker,
the potter from the Nile,
carried away rats?
According to Ponge in l'atelier, no.

That which is very near
cannot return,
in other words doesn't come
closer: vicinity cleverly
separates.
With the exception of weasel and Penates.
Larvae block passage
from close to close by.
If death is the first myth,
then it seems like
Speech up close.
Cerberus guards the country
of No Return
(right next door)
and he has storied offspring.
Despite seeds.
Dealing with Up Close
is called magic
or amagic.
Partly because of
the golden bough.
Yet, should one lose
in order to illuminate the fading day?
in other words to lose the Loved one
to say that she is the general
Darkness to enlighten?
A problem of perspective.
The lynx's ear
rolls the elegant stone
that separates outside activities
from the cave.
For the cave is a windmill.
Veiled in mist.

Red trees
cover many
maples in autumn,

syrup in full force
and without a break.
Hued reds
in packed
gray
monotones.
Near waterfalls
and buffalo.
Where tufts of white vapor
wrinkled sheet fallen
from a bed of swift smooth water:
plumes of smoke worn thin.
Ostrich stomach pulverizes rocks
and twists the pieces
of iron.
veiled.

2. The Luth turtle

Luth Turtle Poetry
hardly ages, we play with it,
and ridicule it;
it is equipped,
and runs well:
like a liquid crystal
clock.

The poem *prompter*
of the world immerses it
in self, or rather
bathes it without drowning
or suffocating.

Let me consider another definition:
the poem is a collision, clashing
against plans.
And the book as well,
from group of plans
to group of plans.

The definition-definition withdraws.
The definition slides
like the oiled object
called beauty.
What is *what is,*
distinctly?
In the arbitrary space
of a weight founding
the famous weighing (of souls,
of substances with sanguine
leanings that we call
souls; or density-*gogic*
decisions). DENSITY.
Who is Density?

Density demands transfer.
The tightening, the braid,
the thyrsus, the olive branch,
the oil.
The lyre is a bugle.

Why restrict oneself
within a poem?
P. is not a district,
but *one only does p.*,
deliberately,
for a sole reason:
things to do
are diverse
because of us,
and we shouldn't
do them because they are
diverse. Or multiple.

(Gather all one's strength
and attention, gentleness
into a single ball,
is several times
the objective.
And if it takes two hundred
years to grasp
each poetic ball,
so be it.
May each one be
like an iron door in life.)

Whoever restricts himself to this
or that wants to have
his faded hour.
Fading.
The goal is to cook
foggy from sleep

sticks of barley sugar
(while asking that the work continue
when the subject wanes)?
In any case, sweets
that cannot evaporate,
always offered
to the appetite
of readers' eyes.

James's objection
to Stevenson (with you
we are in the presence
of voices that speak in darkness,
voices all the clearer
and vivacious
admirable and sonorous,
harassing
and confusing,
that one's vision is obscured)
indicating the type
of abstraction that prevails
in Density.
The type is designated
by one who dashes off long poems
on occasion —
the author of *Treasure Island* —
when he said, in 1893,
he heard people speak
and felt them act.
His two targets are:
1. War on adjectives;
2. Death to the optic nerve
in literature.
Poetics arguable
at first sight
if the eye listens
or if the ear hears
— and this is possible.
There are adjectives and adjectives,

embellishment by the compliant
optician
or precision
by the optician
of indefinite darkness.
The Storyteller's poetics
are unfair,
but the important thing
is the pattern of voices
in the obscurity
they enlighten.

3. The urns

to Thomas Browne

A choice of elegant words
is often bitter
like Garden Cress.
etc.
The discotheque in the tannery
effloresces the barbwire
interior.
Sinister and shocking
otherwise like a field
of roasted
sunflowers
in the rain
in favorable light,
the camp is nonetheless
other than
a dark landscape.

Moab and Edom have been evoked
as regions where torrents
surge
from distant rains.
Their delayed effect.
Illusory butterfly effect.
(For there isn't a waterfall
of effects spaced
between pouring rain
and the overflow of an illusory
anger.
Nothing but a delay
that shakes up the fantasy
and plunges it
into the floating middle of mourning.)
Rain and urns
are similar
in the element of melancholy,
which isn't enough.

And Murphy's law,
good for aviation,
works for everything:
anything that can go wrong
will go wrong.
Due to dominance.
Bitter lemons with teeth marks,
under the grim portico displaced
by time's trainees.
If we are funerary
(there are humid winds and rain in the street,
the air is icy there, and outside,
borrowed hell,
where anonymous bones jostle)
we sometimes do
the rain justice.
Stevenson said
in 1893
that no one has yet
done justice
to rain in literature.
And since?
In rain, we revisit places
more or less washed out.
Which *Scot*
did it
by combining
the old ballad
with the trade register?
It's more than the civil code
or the phone directory,
or than tertiary heroes want.
For the dedomestication
of deeply
defamed
lyricism (i.e. the activity
of a good singer
who delights).
The starting point

is an impersonal Bag
without a back shop
there to explain it.

Sweet, melodies that we hear.
The silent form resonates,
encloses. It doesn't stuff.
Does it take a peasant
to struggle against overall stuffing?
Some melodies should go
around urns.
This is about the rights of the human gaze.
To look on the ground
or low down,
see at mid-height
towards spectators.
There is a lauded
shallow stream.
+ the Dutch cow.
And a wind of
presumed gods.

4. Writer

What is his performance?
Must he
perfectly
reflect the sky,
clouds and branches
on water,
and starlings in flight?
(Beneath the wind
leaves
become a silvery mass
from a short distance
as if by step,
weathervanes in the tree.
Leaves all all:
at a distance
beaten white poplar
where pushed by wind
looks like a cherry tree
in spring —
the leaves
are folded
like white
crepes, whitened
or with silver down,
sunning the upside down made right side up.
The l. of the herculean
white tree
is a glove.
In the light it looks like:
poplar gloved
as if with wallpaper.
The group of gloves
is removed,
turned back into a cherry tree.
as the eye sees.
The white poplar's branches
fall first
in the wind.)

Mother Goose is ruined.
The writer cuts with an open book
and he doesn't copy loyalized
culture,
he works as it does —
it is found,
it finds itself.

(The writer's
two suits,
for town or visits
and for the office,
make two.
The seated position
is modest or hardly gratifying,
the body being in a rather lawyerly
blouse,
for the pleasure of tightening
the necessary.)

Even today's Epik
writer, the dreamt
and rightfully wished for,
works
at working
like culture
that *plays the strings*
to the tone of the times
(and doesn't reach
the useful intuition
of the majority
of country folk,
who know trees,
and not the extent of landscapes
beneath the eyes,
who know what is sewn
here and there along the road,
what the weather will be

at Saint Victory's peak,
disregard the mountain
crowned in blue or gray,
and often only wish
to encounter the blue beauty
of a Scarlet Pimpernel
by failing).
He refuses to have
a humdrum set hour.
The writer writes
and for that
one needs chastity,
pleasant or violent.
(In demoralizing,
how to forget
the hard
stone accurately presented
as well in the expression
"heart of stone"?)

A pure bubbling of conversation
badly fragments him.
A sapphire sea,
better.
He relates to poetology
like a blotter to ink:
he soaks in it.
Well, the blotter and
the absorbing disoriented convalescent
go together.
The blotter takes locally,
without absorbing everything.

What remains is what the ink says
when freed from its excess.
That which is precious,
but differs from the sea.

5. Sardinia honey

Even if Detraction
lacks mercy,
the bitter almond
has some good.
Rage armed Archilochus
with the iambus
that is his,
or: it made the iambus
its good in order to arm
A.
We arm ourselves affected
to divide ourselves,
become what we are,
a generality of interest.
Something in common,
forgettable, dissolved. Or to dissolve.

Since there is the one world,
of dramatic happiness,
and forgettable
outbursts,
that may be shown in an open book
as a type of iambic historian.
There are bloody strokes
crayon in hand.

If there is bitter
sweetness (not fully,
because the bottom is also sweet,
unless there are deposits),
one must still cut
silhouettes
on the partitions
between the channel from the heart to the head
(which is a *two-way*).

We can see
from the style's character
if the object captivates
the cutter,
and deduce the constitution:
full, skinny, pale
colored, sickly or not.
What also counts
is his way of wanting
or of refuting
most people.
Most people:
is a group of simplified
and developed sensibilities,
a herd of presumed
spiritual bodies.
The desire for elegance
is the desire to be at will
a body and a soul
calmly wed:
the desire for synthetic honey
and a grouping of non-critical
Selves.
The more something is *elevated*
the less it upsets:
it is the fruit, this assessment,
of a calculation of the heart.
Elevation is what one needs
to bring about fatal collisions
in one fell swoop.

For example, general raising
to a noble condition,
raising all to states
of genius,
Puration,
raising all events

to miraculous states,
of man as well,
of the epoch into a golden age,
of laziness to treasure,
etc., etc.

6. To read

to Pavese

Who tires and tires
of calling writers
to clarity or to simplicity?
The manure regenerator?
The call
is a call
to solicitude
for the non-writing majority.
Yet, does everyone know
how to read?
For old practitioners
of reading,
reading is easy.
Easy, easy.
They no longer have the respect
within the child's fear
while tracing the contour of words
with his eyes, or his hands
(lever, directional tool,
paintbrush).
He who deals with things
or men
rather than books,
who leaves in the morning
and returns in the evening
hardened
sees, when he looks at a page,
offensiveness,
strangeness, elusiveness
and toughness,
which assails him
and gains strength.

He is closer to real reading,
amazed and resisting amazement,
than poorly versed devotees.

It is with books
as with people.
We must take them seriously.
This is why books are not idols
or tools of laziness.
We say they must change us.
Idols cannot influence.
He who doesn't live amid
books,
if living this way is possible,
who needs strength
to open them,
already has the humility to become stronger,
the humility needed to approach
words with an attention
that is love for the living.
It is a humility that we may call
culture, if culture wants
us to affirm ourselves by broaching
dense realities.
The fear that someone
reads the world better
than you
is the condition
for *delirium.*
An appreciation for amazement
isn't enough. Children
appreciate amazement,
which doesn't always
lead them to read.
They also stamp their feet.
Stand still.
To have culture,
is often to have good
negatively, to keep it
for oneself, no longer encounter it,
enclose it, and therefore ignore it.
To tremble for it
like Scrooge

for a dollar,
is to refuse to tremble
for the beloved.
Many have read.
In reading,
they warm themselves up,
make sure they
see things
in exactly the same way.
For if the majority
agrees,
around Λ fire,
that there is reason
to believe that all has been said,
that the end of work has arrived,
that we know beauty
which is the face of goodness
or of truth.
End of work.
Books in which the voice
is simple and clear
were paid in the price of pain by those
who wrote them.
One may only enter
by laying oneself on the line.
Reading isn't easy.
It's difficult, difficult.
And captivating.
(capture is a poly-
when there is zapping).
The mundane reader
is poorly hardened,
encased,
dead to the soul of dialogue.
The dialogue comes first. Inevitably.
The man without foundation
who aspires to read,
aspires to a life
that he does not have.

But one may change
efforts, change
one's will to live,
by faking preparations
with a lively propaganda
for living and easy
culture.
A physics text,
a volume on accounting
or grammar
require foundations.
Well, there is no poetry
bible, manual,
dictionary
or encyclopedia
that would fully
ease the way
to get to the work.
And notions
about literature
are like fine oil
slipping through the fingers
of devotees.
Poetry doesn't speak
naturally to man.
It speaks to men
of the period,
who have specific problems;
specific general
problems.
Men may
with emotion
or stunned patience
understand that the choice
of specific turns of phrases,
of an inflection
is a matter of mores,
of morality.
A man speaks

to others,
starting with the title.
And the book
is the amplification of the title.

7. Matter, I
to Björk

Matter is complete resistance;
this is why
beings don't become confused.
A swallow is not a swan.
Baby goats on trembling legs
cannot compete with a robust
horse.
Bees sample meadows.
Walls don't fall
right away. Or don't fall.
(Proust resists Gide.)
Meadows are unshaken
by winds;
neither sprayed with rain
nor chilled covered in white.

Some people willingly attach themselves
to nature
for, like spoiled children,
they dreaded their father
and sought shelter
in the mother.
Without playing enough "Peekaboo."
The forest is possibly poetic,
hardly more than the rest.
Is isn't particularly poetic,
even when beautiful.
Calm and shade
may help
get through
a text.
Forests are in many
poems,
and this is why
many
people without depth

believe one must adore them,
give them the attention
given to a fresh poem.
Regardless of whether one takes notes,
while cringing, or while cheerful;
nothing is beautiful in advance.

One could say
that a writer
is the spirit of his material,
of his characters,
each good book
presenting *one* contracted
spirit.
(*Notes for a Romantic Encyclopedia*, fragment
432
also wrongly redacted
by de la Friche or Novalis.)
Humans progress
successively
by quick, quick, slow
like the pure and wandering
eye, luminous, sensitive,
fundamental
(we call it Public
or people),
that gives reason
to the extension
of the library,
and reason to the circuits
it launches.
And all circuits
in the library
are pathways
to seek
a light
or discontentment at least
disappears.

(Addendum:
to Walter Benjamin

A small penny stake
slips into a large
corporeal space,
or an adjoining crowd.
If the images of bodies together
is a bluff,
then lay illumination
will happen as the
sleight of hand happens.
We wait for erudite confessions
to *release*
images still possible back then.
Collective terms
can characterize them.
The *feeling of obligation*
toward Downgraded Culture,
experienced by the expert,
will never incite such confessions.
There is an *inspiration*
in the basest act.
One must draw it out. Expose it.
Reading is a *telepathic* operation
if thought is a *powerful* narcotic
of living screens, that may fall;
and Reading feels
with the right retrospection
how much
the organization of pessimism
is the difficult enemy
of material optimism.
And the interruption
of an artistic career
by matter
must force the artist
to suggest to more than one
what a dynamo is One —
the essence of someone.)

8. Correction

Examples are types
of citations (Monsieur
de la Friche).
The *Poetry* plagiarist
distorts or critiques
past, bronzed,
uncompromised material,
for much may be said
about how to say everything
by some age-old ones,
or old moderns.
In the sun.
There was a time
when saying (in a nutshell):
"Pale flowers for the child —
palms for the adolescent —
staff for the adult —
dark flowers for the old man —
shoes for the child —
shoes for the old man —
buskins for the adolescent —
boots for the adult —"
was doing other
than moralizing
while still drawing from the moral
strength of the description.
Why would that be impossible
now?
And to say:
ordinary egoism
is characterized by:
— a tendency to differentiate
oneself from others, and
to fight to be the first
or patent
a discovery;
— a presumption of infallibility;
— an aversion to authority;

— contempt for non-experts;
— jealousy towards colleagues and
the desire to bring them down;
— disregard of other sciences;
— excessive admiration for effort;
— a habit of finding everything old
and outdated, contemptible
or insignificant;
— disdain for what one doesn't learn
  ?

And Thrilling
in the country of Attachments
knocks on a door that says No.
(Yet, we always
sign
up to the way of fighting
against generalities
or the Approximation
of a moral.)

For Olympic *plagiary*
or to calmly correct morals,
demoralize them,
one must be capable
of cutting them into small
stars
so that we see them
with stars in our eyes.
Great thoughts
also come from
Romeo-and-Juliet
(even if Romeo
sometimes wants,
he says,
to be told
how not to think).
Solidity
your name

is X.
Artivity.
It soaps up paper slopes.
You who enter
leave
all languor. And:
Friendly lame praise.
Mental vanity.
Studly notions.
Lalaland, meaning amentality.
Old Man Winter.
Feathered shells.
Yet,
there is he who lives Extensively,
and he who lives Int.
The second has knots in his wood.
Within,
towers pierce
through fog,
funerary
stones.

9. Hannibal and Scipio

And firstly Pushkin:
His sleigh takes him
outdoors. Beyond the path,
clearing in the snow
knee-high,
then he sits calmly
on a mound of snow,
watches the preparations
by the witnesses
of the duel: they pack
a stretch of powdery snow
so the shooters
may stand there and shoot. Men of polite society.
A path, a corridor
of an archin and twenty paces
is flattened, ancient powdered water.
Coats designate
the barriers spaced
at ten paces.
After the gunshot,
Pushkin falls head
first
on his fur coat,
and his pistol drives
into the snow: the barrel
is whitened.
Felt with the gunshot
a strong shock in the side
and a burning shooting pain
at kidney level.
Then: this is fine.
It's perfect and that's enough.
Now it's very good.
He wants cranberry water
and to climb to the top of the library.

Hannibal like Pyrrhus
that he admires to the point of infatuation
likes to win over people.
Yes, Pyrrhus isn't political.
Brave but not political.
hannibal is above all a p.
And he isn't afraid of Capua's
delights. He isn't tempted
(everything points to this).
Calculating human.
At the cost of a different
deadlock. Historical.
And afar, Imilce stayed behind,
as it should be.

Archimedes evolved at the same time,
rampart technicians
and the distracted drawer
of abacus figures in the sand
("Do not disturb my circles!"),
killed without thought,
before the little pillar
overgrown with brambles
visited by Cicero
who fixed it —
and volumeless glory.
Rain of hail. End.

Scipio polished his portrait.
Without Bad Humor.
Hard to enflame.
Young, he also built
small gestures.
Everything points to this.
Living in the Great Past
future and yet
in the present.
Manipulator, and exception.

The encounter between two
intense actors
from a Center,
dealing with the Center's
dependencies,
takes place.
One to one.
Plus a few horsemen:
witnesses.
Ushers.
Standoff, battle.
The fleet burned,
after the elephants' defeat.
Laughter amidst tears
is bitter.
Hannibal remained free and in command,
due to Scipio.
And controlled.
His soldiers planted olive trees.
Then he was exiled, despite Scipio.
And a new legendary encounter.
Who was the greatest?
Who was in a class of his own?
They speak
and one of them laughs
about ranking.
Hannibal bottled
Carthage up.
Then he emerged from the fog
of a gulf heat
after summer.
The attack resulted
in a dead heat.
From victor to vanquished,
it lived here.

The poor bird plucked
by age survived

his loyal victor
who was dismissed:
he was needlessly killed,
not socratically.
A page without a paradoxical
tomorrow.
Both authorities
are brushed aside.
Others only follow,
and armies.
Septimius Severus then
wraps the nude mound
with a shirt of white marble
rather than red.
He pays homage to the straw man
of the geo-political
Center.
(Yet there are also swells
in the Steppes of Central
Asia.)

The bloody aura has faded.
What's left is the notion of a treaty breaker.
Interesting idea.
Like that of the "beautiful sight"
of the red ditch.
But he was wise.
Chameleon: he wore
wigs for each stage
of life,
in turn.
Shuffling, however, the cards
of Chronology.
A sense of geography.
Threatened because he was bloody.
His familiars lost themselves there.
Barbershop story?
For an acid-throwing
acrobat?
not sure.

It's an international fact,
a fact
earned from solitude.
The sea is green.
Emerald has hues
in the central battle.

10. About a judgment

Who is rigid
like a fish fountain pen?
The judgmental
is the charming order
of a block of humanity replacing
the oak tree.
The judger
is an absolute beginner,
and imagines himself
at a sheer
restart.
He orders
that one starts over with him,
he who orders
and that one sets forth from his wooden self,
chained.
If they believe they are judging,
"Philistines" wouldn't
understand, not
that Matter of life
is fundamentally
matter of the difficult art
of literature;
that
a man has
liberty and plenitude
in relation to choices
to the degree
that he is competent
in literature;
a host of situations.
goodbye gray cimmerian
Cimmerian veil.
Literature: its exact
and precise definition
is poetry. In other words
Riddlery

commensurate with silences
that language wishes to diminish.
For a sentence is rough
judgment.

11. Water insect

He pushes on the running water
or its light current
which is a rapids for him
and jumps or bounces
after the weakening
which resembles the sleep
of the tiny creature's
muscles and tendons
forced into an
evocative maneuver.
He's not *entangled*
in the gratuitous waltz.
The water insect bounces back,
and gains strength from the current
which carries him
and takes him back up,
climbing back up the slope
slowly
or efficiently; he's a creature
yielding to the new propulsion,
a kind of thinking reed
(would say the explainer humanizing the object. P. —
for a reasoned Agriculture?
a slight confusion of *agricultural* and *acrobat*).

12. The artist resents

Petrarch's appetite
made Boccaccio dream.
The second admonished the first.
Some space.
Or Rembrandt is resentful.
It's because material
has will.
He takes care of it.
Rembrandt's renowned
oiled thickness
on the *surface* of the one
Boccaccio honors
with pride
shows that a Gentleman is ambitious.
Egotistically large
Rembrandt resents in the golden yellow
of the sleeve
that reaches the lady's breast; he resents
in what he does.
Petrarch writes with
verve: citations
become punctuating characters.
He's in what he does. Chastity.
He extends the material.
Literally like a filmmaker
even if painfully
in love with
the reels and shots
of his new
melodrama. (For Douglas Sirk
moves within the artist's
material ambition.
For each decision, a sort of simple
drama: how to pose a sea bream,
or pose a squeaky adverb,
re-elegant accuracy
grouped and divided.)

The type of poetry
one chooses
depends on the type
of man one is.
Jealous and passionate
about the oral scintillation
that is the starting point
and feeds all fables,
So-and-so is for example
intensively poetic.
With an *h* if you will.
But, intensity demands
that we bring to light
an embryo of myth,
or that we give life to it,
outline it, complete it,
bring it forth from the penumbral mother
of memory,
and that we get used to its silhouette.
So, the heart is no longer in it,
the Fable doesn't have much of a chance,
and we cannot give in to
the loss of this good,
and a sort of faith in it;
hence the attempt to return to it,
and to approach it again,
or to leave.
That's how possession ends,
actually.

Ripe to the core
has no ultimate nugget —
for nuggets are pocket change.

13. Shale stairway

Functional or decorative
when dry,
it is the anti-stairway
when it rains,
an ice rink.
What if the stone's veins were to fall.
Facilitating slippage.
Versatility of technique =
the goodness of the object
turned into a neutral
harm, cold and unforeseen
by the inventor,
if there was invention.
Irreversibility and perfectibility
joined
in invention,
parallel
to the versatility
in technical initiatives,
craft,
weak.
More than one slate is left there.
Or a horse's bridle
tied with a braided cord.
Minor life.

On the way of being
of the natural object:
in the trash,
in uncultivated areas,
on pastures,
or riverbanks,
the teasel
has a floral head
and can be dried
and used
to card wool.

Sand in the sky
or sky sand:
castles.
Due to mass
secrets
(for ex.: that we learned
too late).
Masses
have major lives.

14. Smoke

Pushkin said:
I stopped
being angry
at X — and so
he wasn't responsible
for the surrounding
Smelly World.
And if we live
in stench,
we soon stop sensing
that Fact:
no use
being a gentleman.
Or rather: we feel it coldly.
To unsully speeches =
to distance
the *smoking mash of news*
often in a letter, or better,
despite its potential
beauty.

No absolute intimacy:
there is only
a subtle erasure of traces
for a *happy ending*.
Orchestrated.
But, the erasure also
implies many *unhappy endings*.
Refusing absolute intimacy
also feeds
a taste for
irreversible situations.
An idiotic speaker
wants definitive originality,
even if the truth
is a heroic ventriloquist.
A synthetic person

is like a reader
or a synthetic child:
he comes. He freely
enchains.
And happy endings are tools.
And solutions administer the end of tools.
With stupidities.

15. Shine

To shine (or aestheticize?)
= inelegantly and through touch
shine, the object,
smooth and straight charm
with embossed leaves
drawn like alder
leaves this way
(the orphic alder
is geometrical).

A house is a complex
case (according to Monsieur
de la Friche).
It can be polished.
And blown on.

Medullian ebony, ivory from Etruria,
Arretine lasurpicium, Supernan diamond,
pearl from the Tiber, emerald of the Cilnii,
jasper of the Iguvini, beryl of Porsenea,
Adriatic rubies, etc.
are legendary.
The challenge of the legend.

The "beautiful" isn't as quick to grow
as eucalyptus from Senegal
made legend here.
And eucalyptus from Senegal
is manufactured speed.

To take wood to the forest
is therefore as clever
as wanting to increase
tight rows of Greek p.

For the forest is massive,
promising the grave danger
of a hunt on a grand scale.
From a spreading mass.
Promising to incorporate:
colorful adornment and rules, armor,
when clinging vines in arabesque
don't blur a horizon,
beautifully.
A horizon of *correction* and *erasure*.
It doesn't wait for its novel.
And its epic poem, perfected,
will be out of line from now on,
rather than horrific or elsewhere.
Virile forest of the crowd,
thankfully deprived of Speech.
Yet, it had speech
owning silence.

16. Sentimental naïf

Between satire (by intense inner
conflict between the desirable
and the actual) and idyll
(by inner satisfaction
due to the agreement of
the desirable and the actual),
the elegiac situation
or Elegiac Situation
lives the ebb and flow
in the banks of Lake Bienne
within,
prison under the stars
in presumed
peace time
(just as the wind's bathtub
doesn't bathe).

Is every loved object
at
the center of a paradise
?
Is humanity
a
humorous character
?
The weekly poetic
fever
sinks
into a deeper
sleep
fed by voices
and on Monday
life
has a quicker
speed.
Shared common sense,
the most shared,

of ancients of ancients,
isn't sound.
It is that of snoring
Sleepers.
And yet, everyone wants
it to work.
Between intense inner conflict
and intense inner agreement.
Despite twigs, home-loving lives,
adventures in nature's
remains.
To *glassify* a poem, its architecture,
is more than tiling
a verbal building (*Meta*);
is to make sure we know
not to enter a place
where the occupant's traces
say: "Get Out!"
The inability to enter
a place without wanting
to leave as quickly as possible
is based on an Inability
to read, or to read
without *visiting* a few
private properties.
Unfortunately. For visiting,
is most often
to take falsely.

Love has had a heavy axe
to slaughter its victims
like the woodcutter and the oaks —
before being mischievous, furtive
and gentle.
In an idyll, love
ends in an orchard
at the height of summer,
with crumbling apples and pears.
Trying out for paradise.

Isle of silk and wine,
where the viper leaves the flower alone.
Yet the dream of happiness then
doesn't dream in a deep sleep,
during a heavy noon where crested larks
are completely calm.
And the large two-handed winnowing shovel
filled with ears and poppies.

The great wheel of Peaceful Night
turns when the vial of dorian oil
serves those who mature together.

17. Attitude

The "honest man,"
a strong notion
weakened by the wave
of domestic dramas,
was a Behavioral Handbook.
Sclerosable.

In the Team Song
of young nations
(update for old readers
and other new ones): the handbook
is, for example, a Jim Hawkins,
who rapidly overtakes
the greats (the seasoned)
and is good for them.
Apologue in person.
But an Opening.
He is a team
unto himself.

I, you, he, she
are attitudes.
Thoreau said during one of the times
of subjective p. in France:
in most books,
the *I*, or first person,
is omitted.
Usually, we don't remember
that after all it is always
a first person who speaks.
He who asked that we erase
"Or life in the woods"
from the title of the Dedomesticating Song
Walden.
The Great.
He was born with a mouth, he lived as a mouth.
To master a few cubic feet of flesh

is as simple as mastering
88 touches.
In a Cubic Somebody's attitude,
there is also, easily,
yet another's resonance.

A science about attitude
is sometimes a science with dotted lines.
Without the dreamt spontaneous
universality. Dreamt by Jousse as a child.
(Especially evoked during
his courses, as young "Marcel."
Infinite Exhauster.
Third person equivalent.
Gloriously fragile,
capable. From an "earthy" environment.)
We don't have to dream as he did;
I prefer to fill in the dots.
The dots on sprouts.
Sprouts categorized A, E, I, O, U …
The tight history of spaces
between attitudes touches
Criticism (the Critical).
And brushing ethnic books
is not enough.
Tearful cries as roots
of music exclude grayness,
solidity, the blocked subtle eloquence
of volumes which are, in theory,
energy packs.

Algebrating
differs from algebrosing, said the Living,
the mothered Narrator.
The paradoxical or contradictory
living.
In Replay, in fact,
I squeeze the outside of the lemon,
with one possible hand, crescent,

and, at the same time, I express myself
or express printed truth.
For the outside made an impression on my hand.
Hand of the eye, the ear, the mouth
…
They re-express the indefinite external lemon,
or a system of fundamental lemons
among other connecting systems.
Even underwater,
using the sailor's aquatic tools.
In the air,
using aerial tools.
When will the human become
a living propositional statue?
When?
He can do it with pure clicks
according to Jousse.
Who dares tell others, country folk,
city-dwellers: "Redo what I did
as a reminder of me"?
He is in "Bassness"
or rather in Length if the area
doesn't collide.
Sub-bassness cannot occupy him.
Here-bassness, or here-bassing…
The best is the melodizing
muscularity, mouth and arms,
cheeks. Giving
figurines, notches,
markers of the recitation's impulse
as a result of impression.
He always has in mind, with his muscularity,
a living transcendent.
Well, he's a giant.

Human stylistics
speak for the Styler
(such as Marcel),
otherwise have no allure,

no ethical substance.
A nose breathes in and out,
whiffs something of the world,
withstands it for good.
In it, one finds the airy page.

(Here comes the urge —
the idea —
to start reciting —
modulate forsaken words —
burst into a Stylistic song —
song of ultra-domestic laws —
Is this walking
a tightrope between both Sides?)

Generalist of the mouth and all muscles
refers to the first rocking
of a Life
as to the first military brevity.
and yet he says
that an organism is made
to rock briefly
after.
He thinks lyricism's
muscular grooves are impressed,
responsive.
He chisels pedagogical phrases,
and they leap.
And prefers output with a circumflex accent
— from bottom to top, then from top to bottom —
because of the body's rocking,
which separates the Yoke
and the Burden.
Hence Attitude-Verses.
Indicating a descent
the length of memory
(from the quick old need
to explain and reply —
to trace, and also revise).

Pohésie has long been
the breathless title
of a remnant of pedagogical sensations.
Teaching in rhythm. For turbulence
comes first in class.
After we dream.
But in fact we still dream
of a solid whirlwind underlying everything.
In the beginning of beginnings there is no Monobloc,
nor a pure swing. There is effort.
A parent may give
a being a raised face.
A rhythmic head.
And the rest goes with it.
He is soon an *ad hoc* dynamo.
Which is breakable.
A dynamo to comfort.
The already beginning man
is neither square, nor cylindrical.
Nor anti-physiological.
No more than the men who follow.
Yet, the anti-poet
is a cradle specialist,
for the cradle
is the unity of the Yoke and the Burden.
It swings in gravity,
the gravity known as living
in which the swinging forces
will not weaken.
To divinize gravity,
would be to loyalize
the swinging forces.
Curiously,
the cradle could be the condition
for good work.
Of man as *workatory.*
On vellum,
calfskin not swinging

in the whirl of fields,
new calfskin or scraped skin:
a choice.
The workatory with members,
the Articulated, the Unbound,
and the Dependent who may isolate himself,
melodies like a dove;
and meditates Dove.
He dictions it, he who is a place,
and activates it by stating it exactly.
He is a place,
and auditions. Hears himself, or
hears what goes around
during the time of
nonstop work,
the time of performance.
There was once the work of the descender
and ascender of the alarming looping
escalator. Chaplin goes up and back down
the mechanical staircase, jerked, balanced,
threatened, rebalanced: mostly
activated, chained,
despite the scant danger
from practical stairs —
still unoccupied.
For it will be occupied in transit.
For the looping staircase is the idea
of stopped walking,
the idea of already being worked
when one moves forward into the space
of the city and fields,
to be driven as is worked
the bolted-to-the-moving-staircase
of the Film
and of the Chain.
The bolter soon
bolted in the air, into the air.
Dislocated, or in danger of breaking
into pieces, and displaced, delocalized:

distraught, taken.
Even so, the escalator is not malicious.

A bird in flight has an attitude.

The cchhh… of the noon wind.
And the comings and goings of shadows
upon it attract.
In the pathless forest,
turtle doves. Demerled.
Disorphicized.
Bepearled?
Without trafficking
behavioral
pearls.

18. Solitudinal

: Grammatical Duel
of the soul with itself
(what is left of itself
from the beginning, is the soul)
or of someone to someone,
or of a group of experiences
with an opposite group.
Experiences seeking
strength, harsh environment,
convalescence of brutal things,
rather than evasion: there
is art in evasion, but when really strong
it doesn't languish,
even if it is a response
to a life in which every minute
is less real
than a sprain,
and where sorrow comes and goes,
Rough brute.

Aspiring
to be at home everywhere
without taking ownership
of places
is a sign
that one doesn't want to generalize
solitude.
In principle.
The Noter who states
on his own:
The *glance* — (the conversation) —
the touch of hands — the kiss —
the touch of breasts —
touch the sexual organs —
the act of embracing —
such are the steps that
the soul descends, when the body,

conversely, climbs the ladder
to the embrace.
Scent — Smell — Act —
is the encyclopedist
who doesn't go
around the island alone.

Baubo lifted the skirt,
an orphic Marilyn,
and made
the sad goddess of fertility
laugh.
She makes one laugh
or take flight
(like the women
who risk mystifying
Mitchum in legend).
The raised veil
creates a standstill
in flight.

Who takes refuge
under which wings
of the stranger?
The mystifying grammatical
girl,
or the intimidating grammatical
woman,
the closed intellectual,
barely open
to the life of grammar,
the interesting Law
however
when one must
establish "Experience and insufficiency."
Aloning towards alone.

19. Twice Verlaine

That there is food
and drink at the home of
the importer of the Odd
friend of the lame Even,
shocks only if
authority no longer incites
going beyond
astonishment
at the *new thrill*
in other words look for why
the ear sees better
this, that,
by inventing exhaustible
answers.
His *nothing to say*
also creates the workshop
of actual literature.
This actuality
I can describe.
Actualitas.

The Distracted by news,
with actualities,
deep-down is rarely
affected by them.
News junkie.
The Non Distracted
has, likewise,
a taste for strong sensation.
He is *taken back.*
Under the sun,
dust in the arena,
glues the eyes
to the ground,
and bothersome
darkness
raises his head
towards a lamp.

Space
creates grammar.
(And in itself
creates is said
in space.*)*

20. Lame market

Lameness because of the "income"
that may come in
at the end of the month.
A lame person is also someone
who stays sitting in a chair,
fist full of hope
in case things go badly.
We're going to the market
to slip letters of refusal
into the market,
washed and refreshed.
The court of miracles
invisible
to a center
that is not the center
of the world
has little coloring.
Yes.
Color maximizes.
There is something to say about commerce
when one has justifiably
disqualified
the lameness market.
And when one has said
one must limp.
A trail: unlaming.

And oppositions.
Unfinishable sticks
(interminable,
or endlessly remade
by the always
Dissatisfied)
will never destroy
time.

21. Slowness

Too swift arrives as tardy as too slow
(Shakespeare, Romeo and Juliet, II, 6)

The great luck
of the slow, in principle
is the luck of the progressive
sprinter, or of the re-sprinter,
not slowed down, but like a tortoise,
not a senator, but a new tortoise
perhaps
capable of bursts of speed and long
pauses, and worrisome
repassings
meticulous repassings, calm
and constant, slow.
Slowness without the laze
of the railway, presumed laziness,
before the train passes
(or the wagons parade,
just like humans and the sun play
hide-and-seek with clouds).
Nothing to do,
obviously,
with Achilles' ebullience,
Speedy wanting everything to happen.
Calm audacity, progressing
and the sprinter's pause
before quickly
taking off again, there's
something,
something to do
after Wallenstein and Hamlet.

22. Antipathy

Some characters are antipathetic.
In them the unity of humanity
and artistic freedom
is antipathetic.
Sometimes antipathy
is just: when we are dealing
with sociological freedom
(If they aren't
"by no means, by no means in art".)

Who cultivates
rubbing the wrong way?
There is inevitability in the deepening
of oneself with considerable impersonality,
therefore indifferent to personalities
and their irritabilities.

We are often sympathetic to that which may
be done with skill or ease,
antipathy for that which
may only be done with skill
and difficulty. Well.

(The all-too famous
mutual antipathy
between poets
is explained
by the tiresome solitude
of sentimentals
that is
by the fact that the poetry
of others
confirms
that there isn't only
one suffering poet.

The unrest is continuous.
For if the personal core
of modern public poetry
is *fanciful,*
then each one is
painful to others.
Painful because agitated,
without lasting rest.
The "warrior" rejects it.
Each poem is pain
and doesn't want to suffer
further from the painful core
of other poems.
The calming epic
no longer happens here.
The collectively restful.
Digital.
Some poets,
representing the Core of their poetry
really make one suffer
without meaning to, by the way,
for they push the pain
further, and make the suffering
of countless others unnecessary.
But each is linked to the core.
The fanciful world is not a tree.
And it is painful
that the pain is
superfluous…)

23. Inventions

Here and there appears
the danger of too many verses
of three times nothing
neither from me nor from others
nor from love nor from youth
nor from anything
for one seemingly found them
while sleeping on a horse
or at the bottom of an armchair
(on an isolated farm
between Porlock and Linton,
on a sedative,
dreaming about the splendid
house
of pleasures evoked
in a book
fallen on the
dozer's lap, One,
the dozer still unable
to distinguish
between mirror and water,
the thousand rings of troubled water
and things dreamed
somnabulistically conscious
or consciously sleeping).

There are too many deaths done in stuffed
verses,
forgetting the efforts
of the distance
finders that form
those called troubadours.
The sky is hazy.

24. James and Stevenson

Two "physiological men"?
Respectful cheeky
exchanges,
magnanimity greater
than manners, and civility,
peacefulness.
The friend has an armchair to fill
at his friend's house.
If he leaves,
he abuses the friendship's furnishings.
James asks elegantly
and gruffly: don't stay away
for too long,
or I may have to
replace you.
Can the armchair wait?
No more than anyone.
Whatever the state of Stevenson's
lungs may be.
The optic nerve is resting.
Thanks to geography.
Unless the eye reads
from the friend on white,
a field map
eluding the land register.
Their friendship is asociological
(if through sociology one explains
the whole billiard game of letters,
and the meaning of blows).
Yet the era
is the concern of their works,
even in the missives.
Clarity and intensity
imagined, achievable,
as opposed to inclusion and confusion.

External monologue: proof
that no-one is ever
born from oneself
like Athena from Zeus's head.
She arises from the self,
for the self has a master's
name.
The bowels are smoked
in passing.
Zeus theoretically sees
trafficked gold.

25. Drilling for petroleum

The passion for petroleum,
devouring the jungle-lung,
jungle as tremendous
as the sky,
and other passions
remotely operated following a first
passion, up close,
create a tragedy.
Everything unilateral
is lethal.
Unity has been named Nature.
Or, returned, Supernature.
Unity has many sides.
Colorful life
has a serious level aspect,
lateralized,
needing poetry,
or structures in crisis,
agility threatened,
analytical.
A human being
is a chemical conductor.
And the crack opens and opens.
World is the plural of closing.
Plural of tablecloths
and manufactured tables.
The cowardly jay swallows little birds.
His beautiful blue exploits, and pleases;
he disguises nothing,
useful like others,
despite the ambivalence
and cowardice from the
human's perspective.
The Manufacturing viewpoint.
Is the sea a stone table
or a table of flesh?
Gravity: a strange shipment

of the body to contain
the defect of mentalities.
The Soiled is a stairstep.
A daunting stairstep.
One must establish
the crossroads of reality.
Burning borders
on land, narrow sea pool,
and in the air.
So who wants Meteora
(elevation)
while hiding the meteorological
(or climatic) translations
of intense exploitation?
One must also establish
the *unimportances*.
The Amazon is important.
It ecologizes.
We can *sympathize*
with the exponentially
fleeting present
as much as with a dog.
Or a dog is *present,*
deserves sympathy,
and other realities,
critical sympathy,
the art of viewing
under a magnifying glass,
of not feeling sorry for or crying about
to the point of cutting short
the need to intervene
(for cutting intervention short,
is to sympathize).

The elements are indeed different
from the child of antiquity: after games,
the child slept near the doorway, outside,
and doves covered him with leaves
to shelter him from beasts and cold.

Who will pump the boat's air?
A reporter.
Confirming silky sand.

Leucadius, Quintillus, Cynthia,
Corrina, Delia, Glycerius,
Names of seas?
Elegy to practical functions.
Establish a love ideal.
A reunion with World,
perfection to come.
Without history = without elegy.
Hey.
Eleg. drives sadness far.
Even too far.
Anyway, it saddens.
Bugles don't break the sleep
of the saddened.
he holds on to the isolated
stump on narrow ground.
Sea is then narrow pool.
For we are clearheaded at night.
Or sleepless.
Who will attempt a new threshold,
born from the blood of a furious sea…
Beneath Saturn, long roads.
Beneath Jupiter, short paths.
Roses on whipped horses.
Setbacks keep lying in wait.
For the even shorter path.

And on a table one may trace his camp
in wine. Appreciating the better path.
Pale masses, who heats up water for them?
Ploughshares shine with petroleum in the country.
And we sing to the rhythm of rural songs,
dreaming of chasing hunger with acorns.

The somber wings of Sleep
populated with impressions,
waves,
flutter silently.
wings down.
Mount Pierus dries up.
Are shadows heritages?
Earth weighs well on ashes.

26. The delivery

A series of books
ties the person responsible
to a special
family of books,
for each "child"
is the father of the previous
child:
a book is the son
of the following if there is one.
(The father is the child of the child.
And child squared.)
We need new books
(in recollection
that the New is busy
doing good) —
even if there are too many
in general
(would they be destroyed regularly
as in antiquity,
judiciously crushed?)
We need others
for two reasons
combined:

a) the necessity
of pursuing inquiry
as in science,
for the more we know,
the more we can know;

b) the necessity to answer
as best we can
the questions
posed by murderous
historical
shortcomings.
They establish a peaceful atmosphere.

As long as there is something
to learn and act upon,
a man must
conceive a new
place or say
something in case.
This doesn't prevent the desire
to stop
and not add
to the Babelian seeming pile
of volumes
and individual expressions
from being a sound desire;
one must accept the displeasure
of continuing to work.
But it's also
that research
is in principle infinite.
It is real.
In paradise
no prolific authors.
Only rarities
without reality.

27. Review

The review
which is an act of courage
often involuntary
is a complement of the book
which is an act, etc.
Many works
don't need articles;
but they must occur
in civil society. We
circulate them.
They already include
the review,
and the notes, visibly
hidden,
or nested,
tight
reasonings, ostentations.
They contain (open
inside the mouth
that cannot be quiet)
experiences
summarized in literature.
For experience
wants a tone.
(A larch torch
likewise has
reviews.)
The tone is atmospheric.
In the sun.

28. The household grump

For the poet
as a household grump
a pudding is a pudding,
and a poem is a poem.
He lacks
equal love
at the same time
between literature
and the absence of literature.

Lit. is not a continuous life;
it is of life, or *in life*,
in aligned pieces,
and regardless if they fell
from a statue —
as long as they are
progressive,
and sparkling.

The pleasure taken in art
is the pleasure taken in life.
The pleasure comes from
the skill of reproductions.
It comes from phenomena
that go together.
It comes from the justification of a point
of view.
It comes from a strengthening
of the desire to live.
And if a pleasure for dissolution
would end the fear of meteors,
then it would be a calm
father. In fact perfect.

(Furthermore, the houses in towns
are equal to houses elsewhere.
If a house is synthetic,

it is original
in its banality
that angers
as much as its resistant
mechanicalnesses.)

29. Heroes

With Ozu, the brutality
of *that's the way it is*
freed from fine
historical analyses
often forgotten in the reports
(the USA belonging
— alcoholic hypothesis —
in Japan
in the bar
where sings and dances
or walks while smiling
the mechanic veteran
ex-student
of the old guy who is drinking).
The antiheroes
being tired,
rather than preferable
to heroes of a special
kind (remuscular? valéryian?)
also work
towards something other
than *that's the way it is*.
Mizoguchi refusing.
Mizoguchi rebelling.

Heroes, they are everywhere
eventually,
stadiums under a sky
with omni-palace neon
and colored stripes.
But before heroes,
natural elements dictated,
more important than glorious names.
Horizon known as natural
forbade Hercules'
weary brutality:
he is a force of nature,

the Muscular,
who divorced her
from peacefulness.

The hero is spoken of vaguely.
He is supposed to come from high
and afar. He is of gloriously high
essence.
He is grandiloquence.
The day to come.
The origin has reserves;
it already began
and has not yet begun.
It is future reserve.
Inhuman liberating
stories.
It founds the wait
for the Great Better,
for it liberated
a man of total action,
a long-awaited man.
Man-response.
Who has the art of starting
what he finishes.
Violent responder. Or a breaker.
Blazing.
Unusual farmer.
Sung verb.

So, he denatures nature.
Bad slave.
Dependent independent.
Exemplary impatience.
Cleopatra said:
leave my heart, nature.
The heroic act is antiphysical.
naturally unnatural,
or a powerful rebelling dependent.
A refuser who would like to

completely deny the object:
exception from exceptions.
It is an All.
The Person who introduces
the impersonal from the horseback
era.
Pure shooting prowess,
gathered in flesh
which could be spectacular marble.
He dies like ego.
And so: has the figure
of the Courageous centered on the self
lost its salt?
Ego equals Death,
the hero, or the idea of the hero,
despite the salty grandiloquence,
and the tragedy,
is the idea of a man
who isn't destroyed
by the weariness of beginning.
Because to change, is to begin.
But the languid ceremony
has replaced pomp.
The Act remains the hero's concern.
The Act cerebralized.
Whether the exploitation is strong
or soft.
The law of the brusque marvelous
is to prompt the:
"How is this possible?"
A weapon was condemnable;
a weapon sometimes has
the Exploiter's proper name.
Or, is there a vertical groove?
Not unless there was a mistake.
However, Candidates
are torn between writing and giving orders.
Pas de deux.
Despite the two aims.

And because of literature,
distant and powerful. Lit.

If there is an industrial quantity
of heroes, it is because a new heroism,
parodied for some time,
risks arising on the ruins
of the State.
For the State signified the end
of heroes' rights:
their uncultivated aim was
lawful, soon cultivated
as a personal affair.
Ruins of literature
create parodic gravel.
Here and there, shelves
where cardboard crowns
are placed.

30. Wakefield's fatigue

I prefer to critique
Bartleby's taste
for the wall in front,
taste for taste,
or calm and dry idleness,
rather than seek,
and search for,
the secret of a fundamental
inability.
The same applies to the bizarre
spouse returning
to his wife
and redoing an ending.
Evidently there is
also the secret of a No
as a condition of Yes.
The secret of a No that is said No.
But a work
becomes what it is,
hence doesn't have one
meaning
cemented;
it depends on the lens of the times,
and lenses also become
worn out.
Wear and tear
is even decisive.

31. Josephine, ter

There is no icy laughter
when we listen to her, or
laughter that hardens
even at the performance
of the best comedians
in the age of washed out,
chilling comedians.
Iah.
(The jackass
painfully makes
the audience
stop
for the fun of it.)

Is Sappho Josephine?
Besides her leap into the sea
from the equally hypothetical
White Rock,
Sappho's allure
is strange.
She is sometimes
an unpleasant wrinkled
nightingale.
The papyrus replaces
friends or companions.
Her legend is more golden
than gold,
on par with the glory
of a smooth joint's
unity with
a severe joint,
soft words
with serious sequences,
suavely serious.
Keeping bracelets.
The hodge-podge
of compositions

is at the height
of the rhythmic
roughness and fluidity
of Held Attention
that is a life.
She is a married woman,
incapable of childish
reflexes,
educated babbling without schooling.
She is a married woman
who hasn't lost her voice
to marriage;
and who doesn't turn her husband
into a musical instrument,
the substitute voice.
The true husband has a cord.
Young girls ancient
like Mermaids
had a voice.
Wives lost the use
of speech
because of marriage.
The woman had to speak
either to her husband
or through him
without getting angry,
saying yes to the destiny
of the flute player,
if the husband were the flute.
The Muse would therefore be Young Girl.
Not Strange Nightingale.
Yet, the Muse also speaks
through the husband's mouth
(and in the audience
there are many husbands
to whom speaks the word Muse).
A woman who composes
is a young girl
married to the voice.

Sappho has a daughter;
she doesn't stop
at nineteen
like Erinna,
and scandalize or disturb
like a virgin
disobedient
experienced
with words seeming like a young girl's.

Applied idleness
called knowledge.
It is knowledge
of the human butterfly,
small general occupation
(fed with derived
generalities).
Mutes push out
chaotic sounds
that, soon, seem like songs.
Stutterers sing
to soften their tongues.
Lack of skill that, in fading,
creates the song.
Or follows it.
Skill has created
very large monuments
to the enormous humiliation
of millions of day laborers,
stammering or uncouth,
before the marquetry of speeches
set in verse;
they impress us.
Stutterers need to express themselves
clearly
by singing.
Needing to speak
in the timbred silence
of song.

denying a basis to withdraw
within, a bubble;
between physical deprivation
and intellectual tranquility.
If tragedy is born
from the spirit of music,
then the stutterer
contains tragedy.
The horizontal deficiency
of the real is the condition
of an attempt
to evoke it.
The one that we legendize,
and call the sum
of historical memories
or collective destinies.
Tragedy is external tragedy,
of the present exterior.
By the babbler's song.
Babbling carries
history's
stutterings, hiccups,
and brutalities.
Little ones know this.

32. My Hawthorne

He doesn't say everything
even when he speaks
impersonally.
The living encyclopedia
of private life
is a succession of annotated
white pages.
Like an epic,
it can't live without.
We see this in the journal.

Hawthorne: the frugality
of a new country (resulting
from *striking*, biblical
terrors – Large Indelible Stains
right into the heart of
peaceful Families. Paucity
of phenomena: a richness
of references (dense wood),
but fear of ladies
and cultural luxury
(an alarming trip to Italy).
Etc.

Which gives:

The moral critically
a pigment
to bind the matter
of lemon p.
If you start the day
to the sounds of cannons and bells
coming from all sides
and unafraid
by the noise when you go back in,
you want to do
something very resounding.

As Great False Innocent?
Perhaps not.
There were first crimes, dated.
Badly erased.
Because you can't blot out blood.

A lot of history for a little lit.
Lit. is very different
from a Museum: in beautiful weather,
we hardly roam from room to room,
amid too many Facts.
Richness is found by some
in the Elgin Marbles
reduced to whitewash
or in the granite of oriental statues
cut to stone.
But, the infinite human body
has no allure: it is the least
solid example,
insensitive granite.
A small country "sculpted" as spiritual,
supposed to be so;
at home in the Bygone Country.
Alluvial layers so light,
that weather disappeared,
weary of variety
a priori.
Old disorderly chess game.
An end to mud and dust,
platitude of a place and feeling,
glacial eastern wind,
social ambiance on ice,
if the work is an infinite amount
of whitewash.
The mind imagines, frothing with fear
that the past cuts through
ancient youth,
the memorized ancient,
dies and that we die

collectively.
Alone on Sebago Lake
around skates, the black shadows
of icy hills.
Forgetting logs
swept along by the swift waters
of the Androscoggin.

The Naked Infinite
is flat,
neither pessimist
nor quietly able to invent
dark things
(for the pessimist, in fact,
cannot invent).
All enjoyment gone.
Even beloved tranquility.
Of course, it must
do better than
estimate the degree of ripeness
of apples:
sweet when breathed in.
Pigmented tranquility
enlightening about prosperity,
controlling hazy veils,
and darkening touches.
On the canvas of men.

Flat is shrouded.
Acute lets itself be veiled
when necessary.
Bark quickly becomes a shroud
if the core lets the sap
run haphazardly.
The infinite Flat
is the Great Habituated.
Unsculpted.
The key sewn into the presumed
Universal Pocket.

Pocket for the lower hand,
black like rubber.
The Customs offices
are flexible nearby,
or a fresh flower bed.
The Big Pocket
is the Sleeping Vale.
If the Authors' Hill
is the Sleeping Vale,
then it is the Pantheon.
Provincial-universal pantheon.
In the Great Valley of Collections,
not a trace of crockery.
Rivers and forests cradle
each other,
in the immense world.
On the planet, there is blinking
of candles,
warning lights.
Even aerial matter,
waiting to be colored.
The negotiating bowling,
and the faithful brutal bowling
(a real tenderhearted).

The Naïve Pocket,
in itself,
is 100%
Negligent.
It is Negligence.
The arch may neither illuminate there
nor resemble the globe
of a very large lamp.
How, in Negligence,
might a physical comedy
take place?
The reign
as incessant
cold casualness.

In utterly dry Dwelling.
Echoless urn.
Huge dense thicket of impenetrable
dead wood.

In the world, in itself,
exercising legs
is the same as exercising
seeing hands and fingers:
they are able to refine
far better than any
electoral biography.
Whereas in the Whole Bag
neither lumps nor mental dough:
Yesterday was born before Today
faded: everything is stuffed in there.
(Huge unused terrace.
Where nothing can grow.
It's fatal.
Neither Melville nor "Central Europe."
Emptiness leaves nothing to be said.
Dill weed from Central Asia…)

33. The unknown

for Carl Gustav Jochmann

Much is published, but little printed
(Thoreau, Walden)

Unknown soldier.
Who is he if he was?
The man in the article. Or,
the man determined by a definite article,
a Bodiless Tangible General.

He isn't — and this is good —
despite empty graves —
an accomplished local lyric poet.
He is delocalized.
Unless he has a grave filled
with republican fantasies.
Except that he is usually
everywhere.
If he were to sing *Domestic,*
he would still be deprived of Interior.
He is the possible main character
of anti-heroism: there
lies the danger
of collective fatigue
with antiheroes
blinded by the sun,
formative roads.
(Sun outlines
clouds.)
The "soldier" with nothing
under the Arch
is a neglected hole
of hard dust. It is best
to leave him alone.
In the time of negative peace.
Where one discovers the Jedwabne.
So how does the Qawwali
transport?

The unknown turns down the pseudonym.

34. Monsieur de

He is available,
likes to dance
rather than trace outlines
with his fingers on the foggy
window that is the hard
screen
between a self and the world.
He is ready to dance,
an availability
(something in a corner? no),
but he risks not bringing much
to she who will dance
with him.
Lady Not lady.
Him, great partner
not Great partner.

35. Blotting paper

A man is a lightness
who drinks, or an absorber
of light. Not a lantern.
He must be changed:
make lais
that give off luminosity
and fill the tunnel
between the inhuman outside
and the inhuman within called
interiority (flowered, deflowered).
Due to facts of life.
He drinks from dislodged naïvety.
The lanterns are outside.
They are relocating.

36. The general rough draft

No man writes rough drafts
except in private.
He usually
writes rough drafts locally.
The general rough draft edited
by Mr. de la Friche
forbids Religion
of ambiguity.
It fractures the provisional.
He doesn't edit to justify
the unfinished draft. But the state of work
that one must approach.
Vertical rough draft.
Like memory in life.

The rough draft is Penelope.
She is better than killing time.
She undoes the weaving of Laerte's shroud
to say that the moment will arrive.
The moment not to raze everything.
For patience may provoke
by limiting oneself.
She multiplies promises
before breaking her dry spell
or rather breaking it again.
Married, she is thoughtful,
and her thinking by a curvy,
attentive woman thinks and thinks again:
she seems to float,
but applies herself to attempts,
or a feigned success,
the Yes of completed mourning.
Penelope waits for the moment
to recover the long-dead living.
About to act as if she were deserting.
A condition of possibility.
A work in sight.

The encyclopedia is the bound
rough draft
of the world.
It is a Penelope.

37. Steer's sacrifice

Or buphonia.
Transcendental.
That which we call ox is something other
than ox due to
the arbitrary or intentional
space builder
of the horizon that falls, falls.
He gives himself up in roaming
the life of an impossible tool
of the self.
Wanting to dig out verses
or unearth them.
But nothing is a *verse*
under the guise of eternity.
Reversal belongs to the history of
interpretations of the digging
body.

38. Mallarmé inside

To be inside is complicated.
One must strongly distinguish
two types of being inside.
To be in a bother, in the hell
of doing something
one knows is important but
doesn't like to do,
not being in
what one does, even
when one brings it back
from outside. (And world = outside + outside.)
Example: the inside preface
is heavenly.
The Mallarmé series
is Mallarmé's way
out of Mallarmé.
Heaven: where
no-one irritates anyone.
For there is no-one.

(The inside fascinates
criers
in the same way as the Poor Interior
in which to return for good.
The reserve economy
fascinates as much as shy
or reserved goodness
to carry on and keep on carrying on
for fear of an inglorious death.
Without cerebrated glory.)

39. Forbidden to be old

There is only one world,
whatever may be the fatality
of plurality.
Gas giants
unfavorable
towards life
are sounded.
And to be researched.
A mass
of solar systems
is a mass of imagined
vitalities, despite the gas.
In August 2000,
we inventoried
about
fifty worlds.
But the world is alone.
Bibliologically.
Politically alone.
In this, there is availability,
the special quality of excitement,
the young absorbing
sensibility.
The very old man
stops listening,
that is: what makes him
pay attention to the thing
in question?

(One is allowed to be young.)
(Some science is so young.
Compromised.
Slave of the State
or of pharmacopoeia.)

40. Bibliologic

The Tusitala from the time of wax
or silicon
wants to bring
the indispensable.
Bibliophile
prefers books
to men.
Bibliologue
resents books
rather than men.
when a writer
becomes what he is,
he no longer grumbles
accidentally,
he is a bibliologue.
Maintains and shakes up societal forces.
"Seismograph of the soul"
and of haymaking in the storm.
At the cost of a series of conferences
and storms.
The paper rumblings
feed the fire
of the Comedian immobilized
in armor.

Humor is a legal order.
In a day.
It is the universe of execution,
but without the sentence,
where laughter rings, and has one hear
with an attentive ear to the possible
trial,
verdict and mercy.
If the author has deep humor,
jurist in suspension,
nothing is said when
one has declared, standing, bill

to the public standing as a single
man:
the great author is a humorist.
It would be more precise to say
that humor is the dividing currency
circulating with minting
received across centuries,
rather than a bill, or precarious
document come from afar, handled
with caution.

(We cart through secured
libraries.)

Worry harbors laughter.
It is more real, penetrating
when it shakes up a known matter,
like humor, the aptitude to agitate.
Yet, the sea nymph
who questions with a knowing smile
has no fear.
She is only foam.
Or, froth that goes on and on.
She is capricious and plays at
endlessly deflowering
rocks, woods, rivers.
Unfixed, laughing, but without humor.
Like Leukothea.
To be smiling, is to live
like *waving* waters.
She ripples with unbroken
breath characterized
by ready made destiny.
By an accepted
and also infinite drama.
The humorist, male or female,
sings, burns,
with some exceptions of happiness.
And most of all unpleasantness

which is the law.
The real tumult.
Marine disquiet,
fatal,
from the wave a friendly moment
around the reef
and from the reef embraced
all too little.
When destiny's character
appears,
the human being struggles
to smile or laugh.
He is serious.
Without which, he passes.
From this the seriousness of wanting
the new.
Counter-Penelope,
he prepares himself for the new
all his life.
And the new will be given
in pieces
in the interior library,
never finished.
Deep down, there is the desire
to not joke at all,
to rest in the household,
waiting, even erudite,
the change according to life.
Sad and serious,
except when he demolishes
the Heavy Eternity of Destiny
without waves
using humor.
But humor is serious,
and the trouble
with water that rains everywhere
on water, serious.
Deluge =
too much water to worry about.

Move.
Worry:
tendency to require
that which is like at first,
stones, plants.
Worry:
tendency to transform
destiny to the past.
Elegy of laughter.
The mouth is closed.
Names of foggy ravines
come to him.
Smog.
model cliffs.
Amusement is the danger,
the encounter. The arrival.
Two enlivens
or entertains.

41. Antiphrases

The merry-go-round may go awry.
If irony is jealous
of seriousness,
it might not be serious
about arriving, and
restrain itself,
and be obliged
to obey.
And obligation does not come
from ironic interludes
or passages,
even if the intervention
is a disruption,
a floating threat,
for irony may appear
at any moment
and return any event
to its *relative*
fragility.

Anti-*anti.*

42. Padded walls

Philosophy =
the art of being in poetry.
The art of not complaining
for being poet, *still*;
of establishing attempts
rather than banging Head
against padded walls
of "immediate events."
Above all: the undefined
endeavor of thinking
of reasons for its destruction
by literature. Lit.
(And poetry
makes lit. dense.
Not that the oral
gives meaning and life to the written.
For the ear sends itself letters.
Poetry the right choice
of every word attached
rather than attaching,
as if the words of the prosecutor
erase
and that discovery may
go on.
The peculiar destiny of the precise man;
he takes it too far.
Some get it.)

43. Anticritical

They say that thought
has teeth…
No perfect book
(Bible)
renders useless
conferences, textual
details,
magnifying glasses.
For perfection
speaks with the rest
(ancient truth).
A book
is nature
at hand
and nature complete
(if there is "natural,"
in the founding force).
Mallarmé wants to be mistaken
when he says, even if
tactical in a vivid letter
to the solicitor:
he abhors authors'
prefaces,
and even more, he says,
prefaces added by others.
He speaks of a *real book*
that one does not introduce —
and of which one must speak —
from love at first sight,
and without help from a third,
husband. Pusher.
Anticritical subtlety
of a critic, of a great,
private subtlety:
it says that *modern* and *poetic*
critics
also

belong
to the loudmouths of the period,
and succumb in spite of themselves
or completely willing
to its enticing flashes.
Public fountain,
lips often sealed
and anticritical flares,
smoldering silence
frequently.
Relationships restrain
and worse.

when the inspired
are inspired
to be sure that words
come to them from above
or from below,
to be sure that words are
from elsewhere,
then they become
bohemian sociologists
often
without knowing.
Orphism now leads to
"sociology,"
to the cadastral perspective,
that engages everything
except an elusive something:
the orphic sociologist
of today
is a controller
or a master.
He is a descender
into the idea.
He wears different suits,
including
the skilled suit
of the cultured man.

There is posture,
but the posture of the ignorant
is either the pose
of the scholar (Petrarch),
or the pose
of the commander
who commands without willing
according to destiny.
Forced to direct.
Doorphone mouth.

44. And prose

Prose:
absorbent mass
presuming overly
fragile nerves of childish poetry?
Today's childish poetry?
Carefree vehicle
carrying.
That which is tight
and airing by poetry,
or the serious fabric
of life where threads
are supple or loosened
by oxygenated poetry?

Virtue is prose,
and innocence poetry?
Hmm.
The world of bodies is prosaic
and space is the beginning poem,
then, when formed, end p.?
Thus, true health is prose?
And poetry medicine?
But absolute health
is absolutely prosaic,
and there is no more *poetry*
if all is heavenly
health (alcohol hypothesis),
for distractions reign
over there, without delay.
There: absolute toyland.
Dolls.
No
to the sheer duty of diversion
is a musical problem.
Musical medicine.

45. Basalt blocks

Today: canal, tunnel
or bridge, it is glass,
transparent, *making visible*,
showiness (sic),
And there again pass
opaquely before our eyes
Filip Müeller's basalt blocks.
They take in light.
A way
of repeating
that the inner world
is so patriotic,
and comfortable?
Or that we would like to live there
completely?
Ears brace themselves
against stories to keep you awake
standing, aside
red coated beauties.

Because of "wooden blocks,"
"puppets," "rags,"
the opera singer Salve
sings facing the curtain with colorful flames.
Are the Carbones dolls?
Yes, in Borowi's smile and laugh.
Who still loves the stifling cries of geese.
The earth ripples.
And dolls would make charcoal
for irons.
But they are harder.
Because of ballasting.

46. In society

to Florens Christian Rang

They said that the Greeks
left a spectacle
hopping.
The paid
to have pleasure
would have really hopped
in a harsh society
(where working is hard,
where work violence
is a fault).
The secretions
of seriousness can
create freedom.

What about Carnival?
Or its remains?
The freedom of intellectual life,
the burning affirmation
of one's impressions,
the raging incapacity to peacefully admit
the changing colorful order
in which we evolve
and to breathe in
loom like a leaping billy goat
or the Carnival caper.
And there is no new
laugh if the pleasure
is unpleasant.
Bad sport, we call
ridiculism.
Its condition: ridicule.
Fiestas are funerals
in the dispersive universe
called work world.
Never yet have real festivals
escaped death in society.
They promised more.

Ridiculity,
ridiculity.

47. Wallenstein

He awaits the precise instant in which he may
act,
for he wants things to happen
objectively, naturally,
or inevitably, without a willing
self. But, since he wants
not to do, he still
wants,
and he loses, from bottom to top,
to the incline.
The landscape on the climb
is his only prize.
The unlimited is delineated.
(Too great a patience
is too flexible.
Changed to a lean leap.)

In front of the blackboard
he awaits
the right moment.
And declares that Saturn
has led the universe.
Jupiter commands from now on.
So, one must go, go.
Night wants day.
Night or the underground.
Unhappiness being
an artisan,
or as if,
it would be best if happiness
also crafts.
Saturn births ideas
in the heart;
he is the sensitive one,
the first to Smell or taste.
From where everything emerges.
Wallenstein thinks

that life is jupitern,
and jupiterized.

Alone, he is sure
that the proof
of the solitude in which he dwells
is produced by his hands.
Despite the slow, silent action
of time
that separates from the solitary man
adored by contemporaries.
Be wary of delays.
The ivory tower
is suddenly
moth-eaten.
It moves slowly.
Who likes a tower?
It does nothing,
falls down. Lived.
It plays with hell.
To Deny chance
is to refuse the distraction
of the ear,
backward waiting.
(For the wind is earless.)

(Enormous sacks of cotton
or cotton goods,
then curly carpets
or strata and veils.)

Is he a self-made man?
Great man
of today or later?
Neither of the two
with regard to intervention.
Probably chief.
He is obeyed.
And he wants to will

anyway;
he is ill-suited to willing.
Hardly fits him.
Acting as one wills is not enough.
Will not be enough.
Wanting at will
is bigger, almost equals
inactivity.
For the idle one is imprecise.
He is lucky
and doesn't know it.
Not fixating
on the Act
is avoiding reduction
in speed.
The fateful decision
is a fruit.
Fruit is then a fatality:
it ripens, and is picked.
Just in time.
The idle generally avoids
accidents. Avoids
milk clouds.
He without character
rests fully?

(Smoky snow,
black trails on ice floes.
Thick.)

He without character
wants to want naturally:
he wants nature, too much.
(He wants too much of everything,
for in everything there is no will.)
he wants to be
wanted by it when he must
take action.
To act = not act, for the demented.

The time limit that divides
already done and nothing to do
or the to-do and doing
is Wallenstein's *home*.

Piccolomini, Son
reminds him
that night is a choice.
And exercising power
loses
the pleasurable and cruel
aspects
of sledding downhill. Slide.

Stricken silence follows the whirlwind.
The powerful man couldn't
continue: struck by a deaf silence. Yes.
(The silent wind hears nothing.
It can slam firmly.)
Tiny little victory
over cherished augmentation,
cherished for a time.
He who takes pleasure in mastering
nature and spirits
stops.
Excess of pure pleasure.
Pure pleasure is said to be infinite.
But it also ferments.
The fulfilled aspires to fullness.
Deep down inward is dangerously equivalent
to infinity
(as an infinite body of a man
exists only to concern)
and can forget
history and geography
of interests.
They are called back to his good
memory.
At his risk and peril.

Does he live independently?
A monk lives differently.
In his eyes the stars
are supreme limits.
As if independence
comes despite
the million dependencies
where man multiplies
until he seems to equalize
friendship and hostility.
And yet,
he is mindful of the priority.
And appreciates them.
Struck down bit by bit.
The ancient brave one infinite
in the eyes of soldiers.
If the decision breaks,
then life cuts in two.
Not possible.
At least, Discipline says: "not possible."

The affair is an affair of trust.
Of undoing.
Of days without,
grouped,
creating the life of a thinking
man. A serrated man.
Without *doing* X is a sod.
Acting
when one can
surrounds a *sense*
that one isn't arriving. Onward.
And Wallenstein drowns
in the field of "not yet,"
he is still potent.

(Who is the best maker of maternal talk?
Hyper-protected speech is a mint leaf
with ephemeral perfume in curious noses.

Twice
is the second take. Brief breath.
There is no more mint in the nose,
in its assailed sensors.
Leave the tea.
Under a pepper tree.
Can one warm
one's back
in the suns' stove?
Eventually,
if nature is reasonably maternal.
Fighting cloud caves.

A dunghill at a distance
sometimes smells like musk,
and a dead dog
like elderflowers.

The candle cures the seems.
And the crushing of the candle
heals the empty pool
in the middle
of illuminated streams.
Crushing the candle
chamber.
It *also* cures the seems.)

Then, auto-augmentation
erases future memory.
He doesn't know it.
Speed stops him.
He brakes,
wants to rein in
the rising mount.
He wants backwards
firmness.
The future folded in the binding present.
To be able to weaken at will.
If he wants. Prologue forever.

Close the open.
Or redo or undo.
Counter the new
again.
Thanks to the inactuality of his doubt.
inactuality of torrential
questions.
All of the elements united in the present
Interrogation.
The monologue chained
to openness oxidizes.
It can't float in the void.
But the charming time
to play in the wheels
has passed,
he takes in air
if patience
is the excess of the imp.

Four walls surround
the Plentiful.
He figures
that ahead has erased behind.
that pulling back is impossible
if he completes his work.
If Self is the future.
when life goes two ways
at night
you must still go
here or there. At the stop sign
you can get zilch.
For the pulled rope
suspends for a moment
and takes sides.
The present yields.
The circled monologue gave way.
The thick veil of the blocked
present
can tear.

It tears sooner or later
especially since we want
to tighten it.
Abundance of the heart,
a great joy
frees happy
flutters.
Pure lively freedom
doesn't last.
If it lived.
an unknown coincidence
or is fiction
(whose fiction
if we have erased politics?)
or is tragic.
The randomness of the mood
temporarily cures.
Then a harsh voice reigns.
Which says: "that's how it is."
Walled up in the heart
actions apparently
belong to the heart's owner.
Outside, the public property
of actions shows, shows.
Heart against heart, we do not fight.
Interior against Interior.
The inside may touch
the inside.
(The household
fascinates Wakefield
for a long time. He wants
to go back out there.)
The outsides, they touch.
Thanks to the vigorous impressions
of life. (Always ex-life
and today's re-life.
The vigorous continuation.)

The Always from Yesterday
is inaccessible
if Before is the Great Empty Day,
the Absolute Empty Day.
The indefinite stopped
by the Great False Innocent.
The Stopper.
All accepting.
The door itself,
with its hinges,
admits what it can.
It receives.
For the threshold washes
Well Done and Doing Well.
A little water is enough.
A horizon is the limit.
Pepper tree from afar,
eucalyptus up close.

There is a difficult step
in diplomacy.
The step of trust
in waiting
is equal to the step of security
in the equipment,
to the weight of reserve.
Absolute Diplomat
severs the past.
Product of the past
In sheaves.

48. The last man

To blink: lower the eyelid for a moment,
drop and pick back up,
reform or consolidate,
to blind oneself briefly to seek
the same temporary blindness in the eye
of the talker; seeking a community
of blind knowledge,
naturally silent knowledge
(of charcoal and glowing,
etc.). To have craft.
Allusions and indirect
citations, or wonderful
nutrients. For those imbued.
Silent obedience nourishes
Culturality.
The weight of slippery
or slipped authorities
also makes an opinion
stimulating, burning.
Since external senses
are gluttons,
we still need
to draw memory
to zones where it may
work,
to zones with historical Facts
named characters.
Apparent erudition
can cause anguish.
It has a sorry side.
But pain and anguish,
says the man who saw himself
as a wasteland, as a buildable
field (rather than of glass),
are the dreaming parts of the soul,
when pleasure and pain
are the products of dreams.

The memory of pain
doesn't cling as well
to the optimistic wall
of the brain.
Optimism is the assumed name of the tendency
to build up strength.
(Pain and longing
are feelings of
the *connected soul*.)
Obsession with originality,
for the new beginning
pure like nature,
where everything
begins again,
is egotism of the erudite
or of the hidden tourist
(but never behind his blinds).
All foreign thought
must be treated
as one's own
to the point of quoting it,
indirectly or directly,
and each of one's thoughts,
Deemed personal,
foreign,
for the exciting and excitable body
is strangely personal.
On the hill in clear sight,
grassy,
the goatherd is cultured.
He is the first sentimental
goatherd.

Quotations are cicadas,
says another,
who sees in the fourth
canto of *Inferno*
an orgy of quotations.
A quote is more than an excerpt.

She won't keep quiet:
latching on to the air,
she won't let it go,
despite kicks
to shut her up.
And quotation marks are panels.
Overly visible do they really make up for
the nerve-wrecking worthiness
of the Marked Part?

The man who criticizes
the last man (his
hypothetical pair)
today
also wants
the Picklock from the Port au Foin
to love him, decipher him.
Before progressing,
naturally,
the eye must listen.
From Afar.
At what point did he listen
properly?
To each, even scatterbrained and disquiet.
Fools are calm.
Yesterday and today.
And wood aphids?
What do they listen to?

Leopardi attacks in writing,
in April 1821,
those who according to him
forget ideas and sentiments,
affection and thought,
in a jumble of dashes, ellipses,
white spaces, double or triple
exclamation marks,
divisions
of an official culture
on the page

or culture risen to the surface.
A useful treasure when he emerges.
The hieroglyph has thus been in fashion
for a long time. Oxygen culture.
(With its *victimhood ways*.)
Fashion of the rare type, honey
or a return to childhood?
Entirely the way
to say *trap, trap, trap*
to say the sound of horses walking,
tin tin tin or *ding ding ding*
if it's a matter of emulating
the sound of bells.
He attacks all surfacers,
the rare Italian.

Olit! Olit! Olit! —
Chip! Chip! Chip!
Chip! chechar —
Tché, wiss, wiss
Johns or Jonathans can cry
on the surface of themselves
and attentive to birds.
They may well cry. In the meantime,
birds are what they are.

49. Antirhythmic

If inner representations were without charm
One wouldn't know how to break it
to highlight their weight.
It would not appear
and a life of pleasures would extend.
Representations disappear
in their captivating ballet.
But charm is cause
for lucidity:
scenes must draw
the eye or imagination
then allow the eye to listen.
It rests.
The waves, enchanting periods,
thrills,
enjoyment or enthusiasm
need a Stop
that doesn't destroy them.
(New line without capitalization compensates the
sentence,
element of conscience.)
Is it about a little
viewing irony?
No.
Milton is light and thoughtful.
A charming seriousness.
Pain point.
Phase.
The radio broadcasts pains.

50. Love

In love,
as in all fundamental,
critical activities,
we take seriously
many things
that many
take lightly,
especially whispers
or the most
subtle touches.
The best
succeed
in aligning their love
with all that they do,
to the extent that their benevolence
becomes general,
their inventiveness useful
and useful
to inventions
both competing
and benevolent.

About
the Romeo and Juliette pornology.
Against love squeezed
into a tomb,
"hello" equals "I love you":
I see you, so I love you
at once.
Agreed.
The pornology of "yes" —
takes up space
in the Room.
With an absence of zelotypia.
Example: both *exemplify*.
Even a friendly dialogue
unable to stop

at any moment
is truly deprived
of a certain freedom.
Monomotapa. Monomotapa.
One must *hold back,*
not speak of oneself,
so that the obscure becomes clear
bit by bit;
eloquence will avoid the caprices
of self-limitation.
From there, he who has love
within, a stock of rare proofs,
floating,
is willing to control himself,
lavishly inventing
outside things,
without taking the chance
of being too limited
when he must portray himself.
Love is agile.
Skilled in recalling
a few happy moments
in childhood,
if and only if it were
neither green paradise nor low and heavy
like a sky that must climb
laboriously. Pankow's sky.
With lifeless sandboxes.

Civil blood stains
civil hands
and the unfortunate collapse
is also in the red fountain
of veins.
Love slices winds
and blows near ears
in the winds' indifference.
(Hence the beautiful brutality
of the dictionary of rains

and winds.)
Being at times one too many
with myself,
I may speak of love,
perhaps with tears
that intensify
the dew,
possibly adding
new rain puddles
to the clouds
with deep sighs
in the artificial night.
The starry battle.
In the name
of a lightness of weight
lead feathers
of smoky light
from the roof
of the seductive sort,
icy flames
go together.
And perhaps elsewhere
love is smoke
formed from the fumes of sighs.
With a lid.

Love is:
teach me how
not to
forget to think.
Eyes weigh
her or him
against her or him
on the seeing scale.
The scale is free from
prolixity's date,
even if love
is spoken of.
Somber and heavy

I can shine light
on lead souls
sad and hard.
And aim true
with a large, stable
viewfinder.
The shooter does not say "alas!"
And I don't shoot.

And if the cheek's blush
is stronger and more beautiful
than a star's sparkle,
it stops the impenetrable night.
The brilliant cheek
is turned towards
the other scarlet
cheek.
Because the name has
the finest quality
as in the rose
or a circle.
The edges of stone
surround the red that rises
towards cheeks of proper names,
without the coat of night,
or her cloak.
The light in the stone
limits
stops before we say
"It's getting light,"
but in the case
of Romeo and Juliet,
it's an "Oh, all right."
Before the fact of their beautiful pact.

Yet, the tomb is also
substantial.
Schoolboy love
turns into book-love.

The gray-eye goes to school.
The unstuffed brain
likes the school in books,
rather than the tomb.
Even though there is a brine
of tears at home.
The favorite subject
rejects barbed arrows.
The gray-eye goes
on the wild goose chase
passionate about Follow the Leader,
rather than adventure,
and refuses to search everything
to find the lost toy.
The precious ones called the brain the sublime.

Yet, the clear sighted
may also become
as pale as any old
clothes in the universal world.
Lead is gray
and can be colored.
Alone-able.
Making wounds
as large as wells
or church doors.
Despite the attentive gentleness,
and the respectful, and respective,
tenderness of judgment
regarding new dresses.
Drops trickling
from eyes
tend towards
gray saltiness.
Which word can die?
Can a word?
A golden axe
can slice a dictionary
like wind,

and neighboring ears
hear it.
The sweet milk of adversity,
unless a philosophy
makes a Juliet,
explains the work
without diversion.

What is the simplicity
of work without love?
He says "ou-ouh!"
"ou-ouh!" without substance.
There is twenty thousand times
more joy
in his "ou-ouh!,"
than in folklore
for children
who are not children.
Walling up schoolchildren
in love
with a wallflower complexion.
The adult-nightingale
against the adult-lark,
such is the night
battle
when love happens/
Because the lark
harbinger of dawn
separates,
and sings out of tune
or creates soft divisions,
that will soon be hard.

Again and always rain showers?
Is the logic-breaking shower
also coming?
Clouds know no pity.
And the key is forgotten
on the dreamer's table

because of the salty flood
in today's house of tears.
Perhaps pale ash
At the shutters.

(Verlaine rain.
Baudelaire dust.
We refuse to put
a final point
on Life
due to dust
falling.
Dust
the detective's
element of adventures.
Rain might follow him —
thus the raincoat.
But rain
clings to dust
and gets even
by weighing down, yes,
the little flakes
that occasionally shimmer
and muffle urban
passages.
The way Teddy threatens
Baby.
But sun also threatens
streams of useful childhood
under the ozone.)

The supple power
of the lover
is like the power
of a member.
And his modesty
is returned.
He says: "Tut, tut!"
to quiet

an inconclusive pride
in vague icy
fright.
The early frost
is eventually
an interrupter, a braker.
Or frost without words
re-vulgarizes love.
Mournful bells
ring.
The iron lever
of loyalty
lifts the door,
undoing joint
after joint,
whether the lover is
a starving tiger,
or a doggy.

Inherited death
is in love
with a bitter conductor
of artificial sleep.
And the gold statue
may be sheathed/

In parallel, the explosiveness of friendship
with its tokens
or its stresses.
Or else: the paradoxical
ivory tower of friendship
because of the life
of writing.
The book is solid amicality.
Of the life
of writings in society.
Of the career of friendships.
Ancient destiny.
Of the impossible use

of *career*
in poetry
(the word
reserved for singers).
Affection is nervousness
from now on;
it is Affect.
A micro of Affect.
The nerves' career is destiny.

51. Of stone

S.: comes from the heart
to go to the heart
at the time of ritual
dissatisfaction, where
dissatisfaction
is coal.

The heart then becomes an ore
like coral.
The stone is time itself
cut off from atmospheric space +
enclosed in a precise
or functional space,
said the thinker of thoughts
form-fitting dantesque
clothing
and the creator of agreement,
the scrambling of words,
babbling *that means something*
in P. (for the poet rounds
the mouth to speak).
Yet, the stone's I
is the subject.
The incisor
carves out the moment
in which to be stone
for better
and for worse,
for the work of art
displeases,
resistible.
Fixed hedgehog.

52. Childish poetry

for Gertrud Kolmar

I'll take care of it:
I feel it heavily
in the heart.
The heart is in a cage.
I feel music strongly
within.
I breathe it within
while being old.
And am unexpectedly
so old.
Everything is ahead of you.
I lead a very
musical life,
with effort.

Why is all inner
music
difficult?

(Which liquid salve might
or what breath
lift soft shoots
or sprouts as cruel as
preparations with liquid
harshness? Which one?
Old silver people, with quantity,
no longer have their sacks of salt.
Antiquated perfumes structurally
fill the eyes with fragrance. Bags of bliss.
Moving eyes on statues.
They go through the ads.
And try to fertilize.)

The heavily equipped (equipment and team of the
self)
rules out the non-match

and stops seeing useless.
Even unstoppable.
And despite "surgical" strikes.
In the Great Sand
Reserve Childhood is very dear.

Chodziesner is faintly inflammable.
Ugly duck
due to Swan-Humanity.

Dry pillar,
literature
is one.
Temporarily
the same as
the pillar in question.
Children's literature is sometimes
dysfunctional,
emotional,
too humid,
dry.
Temporary.
The bite from the drops
consumes her.
Sourness in tears,
that is
held in check
when the emotion
is just;
emotion doctors
nothing.
It brings on
her shutdown,
her closing.
Icing included.
She also has
porcelain coats.
Her pencil is made of
wood from lime tree or cedar.

The fragility of a pencil is well known:
it is what it does.
It's up to the growing one to care for
the sheath, the glove,
and the fine charcoal
to sharpen with the wood
that is the glove.
Chodziesner.
Chodziesner.
With her pencil she draws
a round yellow lantern,
one that turns white
in the afternoon,
stops being a lantern,
becomes a decal
of the blue ceiling.
a decal
of the half-moon
on the sky blue
ceiling.
Fine.
For whom does an alkaline
reserve work?
he who reads the world
and preempts the past.
A ringing of green ice
around the closed lighthouse
that is
someone.
Then pigeon-colored
darkness.
Nineveh.
Remains of the Bible
in the green ice.
I'm taking care of it the best I can.
While keeping a coat.
Henbane coats fall.
For the best.
Who has a gray shield?

Kolmar makes a vegetal
and mineral whip
crack.
Brings into being a type
of paradoxical Asian abundance.
Chodziesner.
The childless magician
giving birth?
Question.
Enviable luxuriance,
lovable luxuriance,
oh why isn't it child's play?
It is bejeweled, bejeweled.

Who does
the long list
of harsh
living beauties
fulfill?
Certainly not the connoisseur.
He or she lives in a bejeweled world.

Is it a matte white
mountainous
surface?
Sensitive to alpine review?
World events
slide and slide there
intelligently
depending on the pencil.
There are pencils and pencils.
The good slider
designs, sketches
black mountain.
He or she may well be useless;
this is secondary.
Or we made sure of that.

Anniverzary.

Anniverzary.
Specific in-ground
plants,
plants in pots
needing pots,
cut flowers
in vase and water,
don't have the inner eye of destiny,
Gertrud's sliced
singularity.
She worked for the Censor.

When she visits the changed place
that is no longer inhabited,
Police Station
very different from the house,
she is a flower on a conveyor belt,
official chilled descriptive
flower.
The Police Station drains
as does censorship.
Before the Action of the mill
or the Factory,
in four definite walls,
+ the thrown door.
Lucidity more or less held in,
read, silence,
for Child also protests silently.
Worried about his fate.
Saintly worry. Pride.
The proud lesson
admired by soaked
posteriors
and possibly abrupt
in the eyes of workers
back then.
In the name of childhood.
For the love of laburnum
on an inhuman scale
that revokes;
and mocks. O. K.

The drenched ones
make legends
in foolishness.
It is wet.

53. The after song

The *preposterous* is the absurd
yes,
but is that which makes no sense
and because misplaced,
comes belatedly. Intervening
when one shouldn't. At all, at all.
As if the impatience of intervening
were glorious and worthy of song.
The before devours the after
regardless of prior
progress, bequeathed to bodies
passed into posterity.
They knew what *after* means.
To sing the after,
is to re-*proterise* the
depantheonized before
so well that the song
throws itself ahead of
the reopened past. De-templed.
And in the reopened past,
I mean the one that hasn't stopped
reopening when they tried
endlessly to close it.
It even reopens in the graves
of great gray figures.
Or rather: in the vicinity
of these embellished men.

To shamanize the epic,
is to give voice
deep in the throat,
humming gutturally,
like the bellow of deer
or the migrating bird's
deep cry,
in Siberia —
Siberia from a Jew's harp,

or in Mongolia
when the voice is *malleable*
and "creates the epic,"
setting or adjusting it.

Hoarse, broken voice,
frog in throat
inherited from the anti-Gabor,
Josephine. But Josephine
also carries on:
she is anger,
extendable to necessary habitual
anger.
There is inevitability in making one's voice hoarse
to grasp
a grain of pure
resistance, applied violently
where violence commands.
A life awry
in response to she
who is truly there,
being violent,
is unfortunate.

I can sing *absurdly,*
in the style of false "Asianing,"
in response to Lopsided Life, and
without wishing
for originality,
the upper hand on those present.
For the hoarse man is well and truly
of the times.
Genius.
Foreseer.

54. From realism

The lover *of initiative*
or *lover of nascent enterprise*
loves *poetically*:
the poised predator
(irritable if
young society directors
are deceptive
and assassins)
has replaced the name of a group
of melodic fops
with a better name
than *affair angels,*
for lovers
aren't at all
angels.
Victimhood.

If many, many
are ideologically
upside down,
hanging on to ideas
brought on by a *warmed-over* reality,
they then believe
they have *new* ideas
reasons for a light
on real life;
they don't think about
a well thought out hindering
of people.
Ideas shared by many
have the charm
of the original, or the freshness
of eternal evidence.
They are however a ball and chain on
the human body. Resistible.
These days, might we honor
pure disideological

retina? Institute it?
The agile eye
lacks lucidity
if its lucidity isn't *exercised.*
It is capable of visiting
rooms, and clouds or mud
that pass through,
but by unlocking the entrances;
shedding light on the comings and goings
of ambition. The wanderings.
The critical mind refrains from nitpicking.
Criticizing the earthy sky
or the other empty sky
isn't the brain's passion,
it is passion's brain.
So, more than one scalpel to see.

Today, the idea of victimhood
is supposed to replace
ending it.

55. Old hoarseness

The shout is a type of speech
that hoarsens one's voice,
and says what hoarseness
says: speech is a hoarseness
according to decibels.
Even if hoarseness
indicates an old outburst,
it is the result of it.
Angers traceability,
pre-datable. Follow-up.

I declare myself,
that is
that
declaration
has happened.

A company
will try to change
the color of blood.
(Reality luxury
will cause pointless sad
ruin: White Elephant —
different from White Bear —
Werther as beast.
Since porcelain
is easy to maintain
in comparison. Or costs little.)

The voice reddens
from the legacy of earlier
voices — takes hold of them.

56. Empedocles, encore

Rather than disappearing
in vain,
with pride he allows people
to not
express themselves while tolerating
speaking to deconstruct.

He forces to write anew
so that the progression
in question
(which is the construction of the self,
self,
place of general meeting)
may be vast and smooth:
and that there be no misunderstanding
regarding
the contributing speech.
No contemporary
is excluded from this.
he seems to exclude himself, Empedocles.

Etna is also
a meeting place.
It can gather
impressive flames
and vomit
red lightning
and make its
impossible visit
pleasant.
enjoyable.
Especially since
the inventor
on principle
said No
to the burning fire of invention.

To be wise
is therefore to *coach* oneself.

The Ingenious Attitude.
Is icing.

(World continuing,
useless supplies
of practical nothings
have a budget.
The supplier
budgeted himself, budgetized.
In the projected sum,
who has the power to proclaim?
The provisions explained
the base of a bullet
at the end of the text of the self,
the Act. After Empedocles.
Resisting the powerlessness of echoing.)

57. Job revisited

If it seems that almost everything
is going badly,
that it is gloomier outside,
that there is less energy,
even though there are
good people,
and that good lies ahead
(even if ahead
we live in
today's open
interiors),
one should remember
that good people
can adjust now
with successive and progressive
efforts.
At risk of conformity.
We could imagine
green tropical islands
in the morning, unmade up islands.
There are plank
cabins
where rain enters. Well.
Fragile paper lamps.
Orangeades.
And Kolmar,
the proud woman firm and precise
in the volcano Silence.

58. Tomorrow Hamlet

The scholar with the crystal
skull wonders.
He doesn't know
what was in it,
sensible like Goethe
intelligently examining
Schiller's skull,
an absolutely dry part
of an elder who eludes.
Given over to hands.
The skull had a tongue
and knew how to sing
before drying up. Respect.
Shakespeare has respect for
a denigrated living person:
James I, who will fail.
The subtle and quick-tempered
Stuart was painted —
nonetheless blind
to the terrifying
surge towards the sea —
as a disagreeable prig
nearly mad,
slouching with skinny legs,
with big eyes
and a hanging tongue.
And Shakespeare admires him,
whose aim is sharp
and conscience neither darned
nor patched.
Hamlet's all too heavy mission
is history's hesitation. He *must* hesitate.
All begins with the
"Who's there?"

What else suddenly appears
from part of a silhouette?

In the principle silhouette?
The tail coat can't suit him.
Even though the jar sounds
strongly.
Just as the sparrow's fall
points to a special plan.
Hamlet's pas de deux
is due to fear,
to misgivings,
to tact and to respect
for the reader
absorbed in the Nordic saga
added to real events;
Shakespeare extracted
from the confused mass
of barbaric dailies,
from the ephemeral pile
of gazettes and rumors,
a kernel of taboo hard facts
added to events.
An unrevoked ball of reality.
For the game does not revoke
the serious present.
The Melancholic Man has a sense
of the game at a time
when pirates were said to be
people of quality.
At a time when the game was brutal.
Brutal.
And allowed us to spin
scholarly thread.

A "this must be done"
becomes Mister. Him.
The skull typologist.
Or rather a Responsible man
knows he is of Action,
a future executive power.
And he puts it off.

His affair
is to do nothing
a pure will *to not to.* Her.
For he is of the present,
in transparent incognito
of a Famous past and revisited.
(The work of art has
one of Punchinello's secrets.)
He investigates. He practices *genealogy*.
He searches through Bygones. Ahead.
The danger of political
archaeology. Of the remote past.
Good and respectable
archaeology paralyzes
the political scholar here.
(One of the skulls is perhaps
an ancient politician's principle.
That of a melancholic.)
Can archeology
accelerate?
He is very respected
at the demise of a victor
who didn't ask why.
The infinite work on oneself
is politically frustrated,
a good infinite foundation
of the finest government.
(Hamlet ruined himself
by thinking that Alexander's ashes
somewhere block a barrel's plug.)

The irrevocable
is the silent serious rock
that shatters the game
and skims the backwash
of provisional destiny.
However, since most
people often need
to "live" beginnings,

they welcome legends,
artificial figures,
changed all too quickly into memories.
For that which strikes them,
is the future, which is here, and its
primary foam.

59. Anger

Among humans:
the shy and frozen,
the temporizer (the *dilator*),
the fitful (the *difficult one*),
the scolder (the *quarrelsome one*),
etc.

Injustice
inspires genuinely felt
anger.
Detached anger,
abstract, automatic
or controlled,
obliges nothing.
Leaves one impassive.
(As once was Kane's anger.)
The only condemnation
of injustice
is formal,
fickle —
fear
of being a part
of injustice.
Injustice likes
a flash in the pan.
Thus, the tepidity
of those a part of
unjust life
warrants
the brief madness
of the body of protestors.

Hating baseness =
change one's face =
change if one must =
clouding one's
facial features,

freeze the burning
face of love.
But how to hate
that which is
great and just
high enough?

The hot-blooded has
elastic, diluted health,
even if he is faithful
to depression,
for the depressed
has elastic, dense health.
The two elasticities go well
together. The easily angered man
has an elastically mixed health
and with modernity he channels himself:
blood also likes the future.
Often, anger is
the violent suspension of will.
Enthusiasm is the violent
recovery of will.
Suffering a violent refusal
to launch.
Persecutors make them give up.
In the calm interior
there is regular desirable
vibration
and most often
virtuous circulation.
Harpo angers
calmly.
(But the golf and carts got it.
Got the harp.
And silence on the
"authoritarian" State
named sum of stars.)

60. Amusement

Who believes one must
drink tea
like we drain
an arduous gulf
(The Gulf of Si,
for example,
where many
slave away)?

Histrionics:
are an interpretation.
The hypocritical actor
had the art of pronunciation.
Performer, he gave
his physical impression
of someone,
a speech.
Funny or a drag.
he needed, as did the orator,
envious of captivating sailors,
to engage the audience.
The histrion interprets. Childhood.
He dances with canticles,
even comical.
His dance is even
sung *on the spot*:
it depends on the place,
scene or banquet.
At the banquet, he can mime
on the spot.
Anyway, he dances.
Histrion = actor,
in other words jumper.
Indispensable pariah,
he is the Unreal
misplaced
in the free world.

he is indispensable
to the ritual celebration,
for the celebration isn't as hard
as ethical life.
Histriony: the art, not of the actor,
as eloquence is the art of the speaker,
but of the mute body,
pleasing, attractive.
The eloquent physique is infamous.
Dance for dance's sake
is external to a *political life*.
In the manner of a gesticulation.
Playful pomp, the parade
must restrain
the Seducer, the Miming Body.
The histrion imitates the orator
using his body.

Histriony: the art of dance
to amuse, divert,
but divert towards the body.
At the banquet, it rejoices
guests who are more or less free.
The dance of warmed
revelers
is the same as the Comedian's
ritual dance.
But ritual dances
warmed *on occasion*.
The players were not
the amusing bodies
in the processions.
A question of gestures.
Or body language.
Hence the witty histrion
that one invented
(One, is Mallarmé);
he has verbal gestures.
The dancer differs from the poet,

he says,
but the poet or poetess dances ideas,
non-woman who
choreographs the notion of each gesture,
the Logic of the Movement
of the super-puppet
called filled hat and coat.
It is the essence
of the dance that is
in all steps.
Whether man or woman.
The histrion lacking "wit,"
as for him
cleared the tribune
of the Respected.
Yet, the orator may
occasionally be celebrated,
and dance in private.
Dance or mime the essential.
The histrion and honor
go together in principle:
the eloquent citizen may forget
his rank. If it goes badly.
In fact, the banquet
is sometimes "private."
In private, the dancer
citizen is free.
Professional or amateur
histrion,
infamous or *good*,
meet in a small committee.
The man with the personality
of a dancer
is a p.
(deposed).
It is forbidden to set up a banquet
in the plaza
or to integrate the plaza
into the banquet.

Playing to play
is = to prostitute oneself.
Create the delights
of imitation lovers.
Playing to play does damage.
For we juggle with silhouettes.
Jugglery has its prison,
scene or banquet.
The game is fire. Normal.

Dance is not dangerous
when we can
move without seducing.
To move without being delightful,
is to jump
in rhythm without the hips,
the torso, the arms, the head:
the top half of the body is too charming.
And the legs must jump
in step.
Spring without imitating.
So, there is *jumping*
in religious colleges
in action,
a specific style of *jumping*,
restrained. Removed.
Dance is good
when no-one has fun,
within pyramidal
society.

The histrion is the presumed
eternal child,
child devoted to physical
play.
Disloyal child. *Glitch*.
When he is old,
the actor is too young,
devoted to 36 roles

until the end,
and already immortalized
by the art of *playing*
a fictional man.
The death of the actor should leave one cold,
said Cicero, for he is ageless
even if he seems old.
Yet, the artificer
can be severe, stern
when he isn't playing:
loyal. To the city.
Respected. Acclaimed.
When he plays,
he is amusing, unfaithful.
Out of hand trickster.
He has fun with dignity.

The grace of gestures
is endless:
it is flexibility, precision,
design, control.
The entertaining dancer,
is a slender and free
statue on the surface,
yet slave
to the gaze of the enchanted.
He has a *disarranged*
and disarrangeable body.
Entertainer, who makes and unmakes
his body into a hypocrite.
The body yields to the will
of the Gesturer
with indefinite flexibility
(the plasticity of a man
without a particular body,
contrite
that of a man without qualities).

The histrion is the boneless
and nerveless man,
for one must have a *softness*
to amuse. Not weakness.
Controlled excitability.
To be *deboned* and *on edge*,
or change, adapt
to the audience,
due to the catching
tenderness, his supple
mass.
For he is subjected.
Broken from the beginning.
Educated to be broken.
Like a custom object.
He is uncontemplated.
We admire him fluid.
Modeling clay by mass gaze.
The voyeur dominates the entertainer.
(In Rome in any case.)
the histrion is the anonymous physical
slave even when he has
his own name.
Could he be intellectual?
Never if he is without firmness,
without rigor,
pure fleshy skeleton, with ligaments, enchanting.
Mobile death. (Rome continued.)
Nonetheless: some histrions
are in fact mimes
competent and rigorous dancers,
prepared for difficult
postures or contortions,
in other words for roles
proclaimed living.
They must empathize
the movement of the living:

dance.
Rather than detract
from rich movements,
they may reflect them
in moderation. Moderation.
Thus the promotion of some,
in principle forbidden
(for the histrion is
the shapeless that we *sometimes*
need).
The appropriate man
firmly meanders,
with neither languor nor gesticulation.
Languid sauntering
is also walking
and looking like the procession
bearer who slips.
When we are rushed,
running like mad
is risking flattening
the living with mechanical parts.
An interesting risk.
For constancy
is the consciousness of a comical
reversibility.
The Constant has the humor
to begin and end
amusing.
Or he amuses without contorting.
Or diving into forgetfulness.
Visibility.
There are constant actors.
Scholars who know
statues.
Industrious, energetic
and timeless actives. Serious. Well.
They are, however, obliged
to go to the point of shamelessness,
the absence of the body's honor,

according to some,
the body moving without shame,
to all appearances.
Spectators may feel
honor and shame. Both.
The histrion always
showing someone by showing himself:
he isn't himself.
Not by himself, he has no character,
and lives *in gusto*.
Chameleon.
Sun, moon, sea,
impulsive humans,
the lively and joyous bird,
light, rich and impassioned,
have a fixed attribute.
Not he.

The orator is Seriousness itself,
and this is why the school
of ornate eloquence,
melodious, graceful,
was taxed with indignity,
and even called a powdered p.
Should the speaker
therefore be hard and compacted,
forbidding himself effusion?
The pleasure of laughter
is sometimes the pleasure
of opening a chest.
To snort with laughter is to irrigate oneself
with too much liquid
or end up dry.
The celebration is humid
and luxurious. Or supplies.
The day-to-day, frugal.
We unseal amphoras
in quantity
when we must have fun

(which is always to detract
from periodic
harshness).
It's because fun
makes the overly harsh more pleasant,
relaxes it for a while.
Or opens it up a bit.

Tenderizing seriousness
is temporary,
and histrions must not
strain, harden, and close everything.
The Loudspeaker encloses
the listener.
But when the comedian
no longer has a place of his own
so to speak,
he occupies places of public
debate
and becomes a Speechmaker
(a moralizer who at heart
no longer amuses),
Negotiator.
When places are blurry,
the Class of Those Available
is no longer called infamous.
Which in no way prevents
humiliating the artist
while celebrating the art. Or the soul.
At the heart of the Entertaining Universe.

For Cultivated Availability,
directed Receptivity,
in a role,
is ideologically opposed
to Action.
He who wants Action
seeks within it the opposite slave.
Especially since the histrion

controls himself at first:
he revokes
his emotions
to play the emotional character
and he is touched,
pouring, by the emotions
that he plays. (As was Talma.)
In the manner of the musician moved
by the sounds from his violin.
His artifice is very moving.
Artifice: the sharp giving the tone
of suffering, created
with precision. Violently.
The waves of the movements of the soul
are dangerous,
and the mask moves because of someone.
The serious amuser
is the man who makes one see
depth in the grace
that most must call unworthy
with dreadful deference.
All his life, thanks to the refusal
of the majority who enjoy accepted
pleasure and harshness
(despite the facts),
he may sketch *strong gestures*.
For some.

The goal of art =
To grow the below.
Not lower the top
or increase the bottom,
but grow
the small underneath,
the promising.
The redefined beneath.
The ex-beneath that is property.
Grown in a matter of a century.

Where is
the only laughing animal?
Broken down
or overexcited,
marbling his head, earphone
head
(due to
the silent
nostalgia
of the pornological
station,
while we call for "laughter
and song" or
"Songness and melody").

Democritus: the crowd
makes him laugh?
Why?
Why does he hypothetically laugh
about a crowd
fascinated
with elephants?
or camels?
The crier differs from a river,
and the laugher is not the laugh
of a fixed cat.
They are fighters
potentially
anti-anger
(if anger is negative).
But fighters
who *appear;*
are they
always standing
laughing or crying
about everything?
Laughing about sad and joyous people?

Without sleeping.
Out of mockery for black bile.
That one makes us dangerously
see everything in blue or pink.
Despite negations.
Silver and gold meltings.
To the fighters' rhythm.

Democritus runs out of breath
and shakes while laughing.
Continual.
For he sees
the theatre
through a gray veil:
he doesn't make fun
freely
of the Eloquent One he sees
walking in the circus dust
wearing a curtain.
When all is
dust, and adds to the dust,
but atom theory,
empty and infinite.
Science that doesn't end,
the line or pile of atomized books
are respected.

Democritus cannot laugh.
We know he keeps quiet.
Wisely.
In a garden pavilion.
He goes far when quietened.
Where is the joker?
Is coitus a funny stroke?
No. What's funny?

We can't do anything
located in idiocy.
Democritus is different

from the Abderitans,
according to some.
Ibscher said: nearby
swamps
make us breathe in toxic gases —
they turn citizens into idiots.
Despite fine water.
But, gas can't make people laugh.
It is in no way euphoric.
Where does the sad or sensible
laugh come from?
From Lucidity?
Rather: from the late
clairvoyance
of heirs of distance
known as lovers
of pleasure.
They are made of different
material than the alleged laugher.

What makes whom laugh?

Someone.
Heating the diaphragm
from below
bothers it
above, there where
we think.
Or first bothers
its lining.
Sanguines have a stomach,
whether they are lively,
whether they are calm.
It's a fact.
The belt that separates
heart and lungs
from the lower stomach
is a barrier,
a party wall,
a watertight fence

or boundary.
Blocking
heat
from food.
Relative water tightness, by the way,
and the vicinity
of the top and bottom
separates them.
The belt is fleshy
on the sides
and flexible in the middle,
or vulnerable.
For sometimes
bits of thinking belt,
or top appendices,
communicate with the warm
stomach.
The diaphragm's dike
prevents
dampening by the bottom.
Yet, appendices
do not reason.
They are from reaction.
Whipped.
Laughter indicates
effective warmth. Well.
It comes from injury
to the dike.
As if crazy,
surprised
deranged.
And not only flattered.
Sudden solicitation
makes one laugh.
Democritus is the scholar with a solid bust
despite Legend.

(Modesty without shy arrogance:
good for service.

Disenrolled.
Modesty is the name of Patience,
which excludes presumption,
but demands assertion or ambition.
Already said under the sun.
Pride excludes *acrobatism*.
"Acrobats" *apparently*
parody oracles. Actually.
Yet, the serious one completed
auracular poetry:
it holds the memory
of phythic seriousness, henceforth impossible
for causing particular horrors.
Seriousness haunts "the spirit of the serious,"
the two fight.
In the "spirit of the serious,"
in which we criticize *posing* airs,
there is naivety to save
as long as we *think it through*,
ingeniousness, cleaning
to keep
in the zeal of work.
There is also in the *will*
of seriousness
a fundamental forgetting of reasons
to be severe; we all have reason
to make fun of the heavy "spirit of the serious,"
to set aside tired frivolity,
the *dandy* pose, never refined.
Criticizing seriousness is easy.
Dolorism is a false seriousness,
painlessly adapted to the *time of games*,
to "life's tragicomedy"…
To *tragic situations*.
Yet humor is painful,
behind the head,
for pain blocks it,
hence the seriousness of humor.
Irony, complicit with the load to lighten,

pain has in stock.
Today's orphic complainant
left old hymns behind early on.
Today's humor is glacial:
ice age of singers
but
for the last two centuries,
before the thaw.
For tertiary "heroes.")

61. To do like Williams

The hanging doctor,
hanging when he writes,
chose
the sour grapes motif.
He always defined
the poet (in himself or elsewhere)
as a man *without* success,
if it isn't in his head,
and his head, is devoted
to something
entirely different
from what we call Arrival, success.
He has his briefcase.
The poet puts his heart
into what he does
and if he succeeds with the poem
then *it's* a success.
Sour grapes
are as beautiful
as the regular kind.
My bunch of grapes
evokes beauty
with its type of roundness,
as much as any
bunch of grapes,
sour or sweet.
To do like Williams: adapt
to the interrupted banality
of life.

It is normal
to turn against
someone who doesn't have success.
Success makes one capable of success,
as genuinely *selfic*
in itself
as defeat (private defeat).

Lack of success removes its possibilities
from the man who was doing well,
or for whom things
were going.
Not only
the public sees
the confident walk
of the man who does the difficult,
but the renowned man
also sees it;
he knows his strengths.
In the same way, he is capable of seeing
the faux pas.
Success makes the wrestler beautiful,
and generous and sure,
it polishes hypocrisy.
Lack of success defeats, erases
or soaks
the example's face.
The achievement of the best
is as interesting
or suspect
as failure.

The idea of profession
is also the idea
of difficulty.
Peeled.
With Yesses.

62. Virgil's modesty

Just as Racine's tragedy
begins with order or the need to stop,
so the epic poet is
often the celebrated trumpet:
Virgil in the unredacted beginning
of his song is modest,
ill-at-ease and brave,
and says that he relies on the muse.
That he added, as said,
a trumpet-free beginning,
which he published then rejected
in private, matters not:
La Fontaine is already in Virgil,
for the fable recaptures,
rather than the swelling of the epic,
its modest, beginning or
brave impulse. He says (there is always
a "he says" in genius):

some time ago
I modulated my song
on a fragile, thin or slender pipe,
before feeling the horror
of arms and the man
who suffered tragically from them,
due to an anger of which the Muse
should tell the cause.

63. Museum

He says that a word wizard
is deprived of a home, or that he lives
in shadow-filled woods,
and that he hangs around calming banks,
prairies refreshed
by streams;
that he can show luminous
plains
to those who ask.
According to him, he is the solution.
But without pain.
Only with the charm
of the music coming
from an arranged elder wood.

Orphic head of the anticipating
and procurating prophet,
Great Replacement
of the Future and of Elevation,
is reduced to hollow-headed
speaking doll,
resonating the drone
of a small plane, the captive fly,
born from heat.
The Thracian is cold
and extinguishes as much as he lights.
Realities are candles.
He lives inertia
and sees that shadows are stiff.
But he sings his own destiny —
see that inertia
is outside:
he is danger.
He is danger, for he senses
and says that at the core of each and all
there is something deeper than blood
or laughter:

a trace.
A person with character
knows how to repeat himself;
in fact, he repeats himself
with consistency.
His destiny even, unified,
drama-free.
A person without character
hence has a destiny.
His life is dramatic,
circuitous, and juristic.
For law is demonic,
an insurer, a binder,
a guarantor.
Tragic destiny can shake up
the assuring genius.
And so, the hero is the genius
who seeks syllables
to justly answer
violence from above,
the menacing vertical
law.
A jurist.
But he is the moral man
and voiceless
who seeks righteousness.
Genius is everything but owner
of destiny:
the judge determines
the destination.
And assaulted Genius
cannot abdicate.
He begins and carries on.
The comedian escapes destiny,
flees from judgment. In theory.
He constantly characterizes himself.
And may then freely persist.
Is this possible?
Tragic action

has a comic shadow.
Action is deprived of comedy.
Due to the voice's destiny,
the Thracian breathes hot
and cold.
Deprivation justifies smiling.

64. Sunflower

to Villon

The tongue turns
once
each time.
It can
make plans
when it is the only
practice of a man
who turns and returns
phenomena
in phrases.
And in phrases
we pick up frozen words
to warm them
between palms
that are also phrases;
and in their thawing
we truly hear them.
The cold water
poured
by the Universal Parliament
of hearts-in-heads,
which is melted snow,
is still cold
for a moment.
The soluble ice of days gone by
is the seasonal one,
the recent one that will soon
return, and that will soon
be the idol
who returned from the past
that we mourn
when he is again
solidified in the present
before melting once more
in sadness.
Fooled.

Hence the malcontent
who adds
to official speeches
drunk daily
and held by Herr Omnes.
Add = melt
ice
by inserting the sun
into the heart channel
in the head,
which controls
dexterity.
Dexterity
turns stanzas
like sunny
snowballs.
So

reheated snow =

(spectacle) little pan of ice
(large crystal,
like a chunk of salt)
melted, and melting
along the window pane
(or windshield
and northwind-shield)
leaving a dribble of old ice
and new
along the slow slide,
in the morning under
a pale or vivid sun,
ahead of the new school.
Modest *show.*
The windshield wiper stopped.
No never-ending snow.
No more.
And now (announces):
The end of Kilimanjaro.

Well, well.
Behavioral or
environmental p.
has warmed up.
Their climatic change
is that of heads
or hearts.
Well.
Hmm.
In whom is the sea frozen?
In climaterics.

65. Dialogue with Leuco

If the poet
avoided
wanting to build
a myth…
Between person and imperson.
Pavese speaks of unique places
fresh, available,
not of a particular place;
rather of those with names
that are common, vague,
first:
the meadow, *the* cave, *the* forest
perhaps wild
(where trees free themselves),
the beach. Even *the* house.
It was there. Here is different.
Set places, unspecified,
reminiscent of similar places.
All the same places.
Of focused travel. Rentals.
These unique and expressive places
can be called mythical.
Captivating generalities.
Creating them without claiming them.
Where one could.
To Myth, is to do this or that
once and for all. And to *found.*
Whence the immaterial guidance
(or material by scribes).
When the tireless demolition of myths
is the founding myth,
the only core attracting a pen pusher,
what's left is Suicide.
The set standard will set him
for good. He thinks he'll
reach Longed for Clarity.
(At the center of a land.

The underground from Iceland to Italy
is decreasing just so.)
The mythical hard core
of the solitary
man
is fictional, disturbed:
no-one rests there
like we lie down in the Epic,
especially not the future Member
of Society.
End of a painful
versatility of life.
Invaluable versa.
He will be the sole old wicker
weaver, having stopped
practicing
his profession. He wants to quell
his fever for uniqueness.
The juices are absent when "twice"
is the second time. Before, the "first
time" could, when feverish, be lived
and relived. The "first time"
is the only powerful tonic
but the *remything* demolisher of myth
prepares himself to tire of
drinking any. Beverage of depths.
Cordial.
The Core, is the Abyss.
Before giving up, the lover of painful
and exhausting longing will sometimes
do as he wishes.
Already dazed by the hotbed of first
stupors.
Prehistoric admiration is tragic here.
The feverish man suffers thoroughly.
Due to myth; the availability
of a primary identified story
deep down always a bit obscure
and birthed from individuality.

He wants to swim in it, that is smoothly
repeat gestes over and over
with renewed impetus and frothy play.
He wants to tell and tell,
loop the already inevitable bottom,
swim and swim in a big blue
of blue past. With whirlpools
in the flow, surfacings,
victorious jubilation,
lamentations summarizing a past.
The monotonous song of the breaststroke swimmer
or mythical crawler
must haunt individualities.
For the singular swimmer,
who willingly repeats himself,
is haunted by Generality.
And the transmission or communication
of a depth nevertheless closed,
closed to all, which must fascinate.
Create People. Seek.
The exemplary depth since
the permanence of a self after Homer
and the collectivers
is presumed appealing; we feel it,
and we clarify the feeling
of being important deep down. Captivating.
(We put an end to the self
with the final point of pure enlightenment
in a gunshot,
in the thrust of Mishima's sword.)
A life may consider itself
complete. Become *a priori*.
Even infinitely frustrated
it can seem
essential and familiar,
rhythmic destiny, the thread of the future,
a path to follow.
A Path: that which brings something.
Until dawn, or worry.

Reality is the web of mythical
events turned into enlightened stories.
And if they are pure clarity,
they stop saying anything.
So does myth alone say something?
He who cannot be confined
without writing? Who can't stand cotton?
Or nonstop limelight?
Myth leading
to the Great Fatigue
is one from the ashes of days,
where ember is desire.
For at the end, it is indeed rarity
that is grieved.
Scarcity may then fascinate
smooth talkers,
and like angel masks,
they want to go back
after the back-and-forthing
of progress and naïve returns.
And no inlays at all anymore.
Yet maturity makes
good use of hands and the brain.
In childishness a preference for the bud,
despite the irreducibility
of primary facts,
or of the flower in full bloom.

The bottom is the bitter nymph.

So:
The noter = a kibitzer?
The k.
has his say
and as long as it is said
naturally,
foolish is he who comments
on the lives of men
close to him
to improve them

perhaps,
or some sort of genius.
Encruster.
Man nourished
and nutritive.
Player alongside player.

66. Beasts

Who wants
us to be a divided
assembly of plant
and ghost?
Buffon says
that animals,
rather than gaining strength,
on the contrary lose it
bit by bit.
Time works against them.
The more the human species
multiplies, perfects itself,
the more animals feel the weight
of a power as terrible
as it is absolute,
barely leaving them
individual existence,
and removing from them the idea
of liberty, society,
intelligence.
What they were,
what they will become
neither points well
to their past
nor their possibilities.
We don't know,
if humankind
disappeared,
to which of them
would belong
the power here;
in which muddy or clear
river.

67. A clarification

Classical prowess
(which is also a matter of class)
was sometimes to renounce revolt
at the price of courage
due to a change
of circumstances.
The feat is to calmly
foresee
the farmer's glory
and to change
action accordingly.
The clear and supple anger
of the "classical future"
(future, for its future
is a matter
of class,
if scholastic textbooks
hide it)
is no less alive
than anger that revolts.
On the contrary: the effort
of No is in the movements
liberated by poise.
It, poise, is true to
the Mythical Zero
if it *forbids*.

The reserved silence of hoped for,
and calmly respected history,
can entail rightful sobriety.
The imminence
of another quality of silence
is also a vacuum
filled with indefinite radicalism.
The will to clarify,
for earthly sobriety,
of Laverie,

escorts the desire for naivety
or the erasing of traces
on the surface of publications.
But irony is the forgotten
and long-lived phantom
of natural appearances
or of sentences
due to endless
alternating
of self-creation
and self-destruction
that is the law
of impressive
ancient literatures
(sources from which
we want to drink again
when the air
is too warm in life
with those from the same time).
For the warmth
is due to the same
life's irony
as in the time when
the Great Naïfs
stuffed their writing
with well-felt allusions.
So, the irony
antirhythmic capability
is the ability to twist
images so that we see
what it is;
to progress from an evoked élan
to an evoked élan.
(Hence the importance
of Warburg.)
Violently contracted facial muscles
destroy beauty
even from the orgy contained
in calm;

and the unfinished atlas
of poses bearing the marks
inverts the energy of muscles.
But is there a conservatory of poses?
Is there a list of actions,
the beginning of a classification:
brutal triumph, avid pursuit,
radical grievance
??

68. Matter, II

Plebe expressions
suit when needed
in the wood of the real
to express, or to press.
The anodyne liquidambars
of the schoolyard
stand there,
and suggest that wood
requires examination.
Carbon wells
against the progressive
tearing of the layer
in the sky.
Reps.

And we say: X is the beginning
and the matter of a manufacturer.
It isn't an entire
manufacturer.
In his works, there are
beginning and
half-able parts.
It's a big murky
and muddy spring.
discharging sludge
and silt,
where the water disappears
bit by bit,
once it starts to run.

Yet, the big spring
continuously carries and carries
because of the rational
boasting
of matter.
Who is matter
as was a singer,

in principle,
the Voice?
From crushed water lily
to crushed water lily?

69. Ignorance of X

The radical idiot
as absolute
dangerous
start over
of civilization
is exemplary?
He differs from he who,
ready to cross the threshold
into historical disappearance,
answers one more time,
a shadow
the call to dive
there where one arrives with difficulty:
the new for the era.

Boredom is hunger,
and the need to replace
bores.
Without needing
to replace, the era also
flees.
"The phooey-est role
in a fffuuiie film" (Pialat)
also matters
if it needs this or that.
The "vraoumpteufpteufbrraoum"
(Pialat), in other words the motor
in no way guarantees the utility
of the automobile,
if a work is an automobile,
for example.
Does it have per se the principle
of its mobility?

The fascinating one:
turns a type of beam
and others operate

the belt that they hold
by both ends
while the wick turns
sharpening the stake
under the flame,
and the stake, the sharpened beam,
burns.
Fervor grills,
eyelid and eyebrow sizzle,
like roots or little
vision pipes.
Like an axe
or wagoner's axe in cold water,
when the metal whistles,
the olive tree stake blinds or kills
the big guy who forgets
to look where he should.

Childhood, as often as
that of little ones
(who are Antiques,
and real children
are not),
is a mumbling
that man twists,
turns serious.
It's a matter of the mature man
who scowls and yawns.
Baffling and forbidden
stammering,
without the illiterate virtue
that some like.
Yet, a child may well
challenge
his casualness
and press a finger
on his lips.
(lips = parts
of a telegraph,

and little
brothers to the eyes,
if we will,
able to open
and close,
lashes below,
eyelashes or eyelids
of the mouth
for which the forehead is,
if we will,
the nose,
the forehead-forehead
being in a way
the eyes' nose —
for the eyes —
telescopes —
and nose
have their own horizons,
very distinct.
Man = immense mass of clay
partially sunken.
The hand, possible ancient
large palm leaf
with lobes and veins?
The ear, lichen or side
navelwort, with a possible
large lobe?
The lip in movement
goes over the sides
of the "mouth cave,"
making a small cave
now.
The nose, frozen stalactite,
a drop from a sizeable mass
under a clement sky
where thaws take place?
So, Chin, a larger drop,
confluence of the Face's currents.
Cheeks, two landslides

from the forehead towards the miniature
valley
of the Face,
and the cheekbones separate the currents.)

Stretched like steel on an anvil,
a work is soon
a camel's load,
kilos of lead or feathers.
The *styler*
provides
an amagical and incisive
or inciting
x
while enclosing it
the way we ship fruit
in a silver container
wrapped in a cloth
which will please people.

We must speak of need
with need,
of Brittany's whale
or of the dolphin,
or of a double cloud,
the battle between ignorance
and ignorance,
or of Laberius, the ancient knight
made mime at Caesar's calm
and firm request.

Humans are the same as owls
perceiving light
blinded by the sun.
We celebrate the sun,
absent friend,
with words.
But the hand cannot hold
the sky

like a quill.
The sky is wrongly compared
to the inkwell
(and the Self is also
decreed gold or
silver mine);
we call
emerald green,
snow white,
a raven black.
Where happiness
has nothing to do
with the ship
seen by the shepherd
from mountain top,
when he imagines
that it is a rock
emerged from the earth
and pushed
with the wind's power,
then hears the people
who operate the ship,
the song of sailors
approaching,
and rolls thoughts around
in his head,
and sees that the rock
is not a rock.

The ignorant person who wants to know
is in a boat
amidst the currents
of the Po.
He also has grapnels and ropes
to advance under a colorless sky.
Longing makes many
tools useless.
It has been said that it crawls
like a snake

or attacks the roots
of glories and of names,
or that it looks like
earthworms
whose clandestine bites
secretly
eat away at
the high trees in the mature forest.
Venom strikes soundlessly.
But longing sometimes
foams
and suffering then shatters the silence,
that of real consular fools,
that of scholars jealous of scholars
(in this jealousy by the way
it seems like a sea that swells,
or inflates, from the silence
of winds).

We sometimes say
that a grown-up
is sand without cement
or an arena
without a finish line,
an infinite track.
Well. Alongside virtuous circles.
He holds only
his reason captive.
Imagination
makes one irritable,
arrogant
and difficult,
unlike that of
MacWhirr,
whose face
betrays
neither silliness
nor firmness.
(And even a man

without qualities
or almost
can have
a father with qualities.)

70. Islands

to Keats

Do you not hear the sea?

(Shakespeare, *King Lear,* IV, 6)

Work of waves
or of a statuary,
space and time
are the world's angels,
risked someone
for whom
"paradise scatters here."
OK.
We should also write
on the gate of the illustrious Paradise
what Dante wrote
on the gate of Hell:
Abandon all hope,
ye who enter here.

And if we want to imprint
impressions of nature
such as
describe the soft sound
of raindrops,
we remember that this sound
might also please
the roofless.
The land of roofs is not
by the way
the land of toys.

Can the atomized
have
a strong
interest
in things,
or feel

exactly
the trembling of a leaf,
the color of a blade of grass,
aspects of a clover,
the buzzing of a bee
like a little airplane,
or the splash of the drop of dew
in its lighting,
the sigh of the wind,
the odors that come
from the forest,
anyway One After the Other
the exact rhapsody
of things?
(August Bedloe
holds a thousand centuries
within him.)

Permanent
murmurs
surround
the beaches,
and the heave
powerfully
fills the caves.
Mildness often comes
from calm,
and the pearly seashell
stands still
for days and days
before washing ashore
on the sand
when the stillness ends.
Who hibernates?

Irritated, weary,
we walk the shore.
Ears hurting
we slide soundly

on the sand.
And those who are
also less tied
to the town
(I don't say:
"populous,"
Milton)
find
flint and iron.
And a life of responsible
emotions.

Melancholy reigns
due to the difficulty
in being worthy,
in other words
overcome oneself.
(Or overcome the Annoyances that gather within us.)

The island feeling is cubic. —
Are there two business minds?
two types of business men?
From one island of feelings
to another island of feelings, we should
pass, or jump:
life is sporadic, titanic
water,
seemingly lacking cohesion, water
and bridges.
Life is colors,
sounds and strength.
It has members.
In a typhoon,
rescuing the impersonal
obliges. Obliges.

The Midas touch
changes, the saying goes,
things to gold:

especially the sun
for whom realities,
the saying goes,
are beautiful.
Sun is the golden touch.

Class relations disappear
in death, we say.
Ideo-, ideo-,
Who wants
to graze death? What idiot? Re-die
once passed, continue
to kill oneself without stopping, irritate oneself
infinitely
without irritability = stop oneself
before starting. Unplugged,
don't upset, and deactivate oneself.
In a circle without hostility,
there would be a circle of Complete Individuals,
Absolute Floating Islands,
or Sheets that float,
for calm phantoms
are enemies,
never hostile nor veiled,
perpetuities, pure individuals
who don't care much to seduce,
for off the coast of the islands
up close,
never brushed against, or rubbed up against, "touched."
One doesn't eat there.
One doesn't build there
three seconds of modeling
clay each day
for the film.
So, bodies are more fragile
than the paper prison
in which children enclose flies?
No paradise is fierce.
Where one would blow on
the milk of Muses.
No iota, theta, fleita, flute.
Nor self-praise from the cathedralist,
from the guild of p., warden
in charge (presumably) of the whole man,
with related obligations, secular,

his contracts, body, attitudes,
capable of, as the Cremone guild could
destroying recanted paintings,
demolishing disqualified poems.

But then again:

there wouldn't be
— 24 sports events per polar night;
— hours, like a distant great castle;
— deaf and forgetful humans
(all past, all present forgiven).

Nothing but:

General floating of silhouettes.
Ethereal floating.

Let's observe the type of warm-up
called inspiration.
With the necessary cooled down,
muscular force enters
rather than nervous emotions.
The nerves send Warm Lucidity.
Up to the Rooms of International
Mobility
or to the Rooms of the Creative Interior
the first time is forgotten.
These are havens.
Elsewhere, cure nostalgia with vaccination,
by inoculation of doses of nostalgia
with the "industrial poetry"
of advancers. Who know.

Lunapark was a sanitarium,
for healing at the speed of nature;
by recovery of contact with Nature at the fair.
Silhouettes rub shoulders there.
Song-lovers despite Hollerith's machine;

nutshells of civility. Yes.
They remember speed.

The agonizing reed flutes,
sometimes solely plunging into mourning.
It is frequently full of praise. Civility.
In alas *there is praise*
for the recent soon.
For soon signifies passage.
And of the motivational.

June 2000 – August 2001

The Groove of the Poem: Reading Philippe Beck
Jacques Rancière

A careful reading of one of France's most important contemporary poets by one of today's most engaging thinkers of aesthetics.

Grafts: Writings on Plants
Michael Marder

A vital call for the cross pollination of philosophy and plant sciences.

A Love of UIQ
Félix Guattari

An exciting attempt by one of France's most well known thinkers wherein he explores his thought through the form of a cinematic narrative.

Desert Dreamers
Barbara Glowczewski

An ethnographic adventure exploring the Warlpiri and their cultural practices of "the dreaming" in relation to their societal laws, ritual art, and connection with the cosmos.

Cartography of Exhaustion: Nihilism Inside Out
Peter Pál Pelbart

A meditation on the possibility of fighting off the exhaustion of our contemporary age of communicative and connective excess.

Other Univocal Titles

Univocal Publishing
411 N. Washington Ave, Suite 10
Minneapolis, MN 55401
www.univocalpublishing.com

ISBN 9781937561680

Jason Wagner, Drew S. Burk
(Editors)
All materials were printed and bound
in September 2016 at Univocal's atelier
in Minneapolis, USA.

This work was composed in Garamond.
The paper is Hammermill 98.
The letterpress cover was printed
on Crane's Lettra Fluorescent.
Both are archival quality and acid-free.